ANSWERING COMPASSION'S CALL

The Serrano Family

"I am always reminded of how our Heavenly Father gets things done. It is not about buildings, homes, schools, clinics, or churches, because one day all of these will fade away. It is Him building His dwelling place within us, and Him doing what only He can do in us. He is saving, restoring, and rebuilding what cannot be done with human hands. He does not build dollar to dollar or brick to brick. Our Father builds Heart to Heart."

Amy Serrano, Founder and Director
Worldwide Heart to Heart Ministries, 1998-2018

Oscar Serrano, Amy Serrano, Mary Frenter, Lyle Frenter

"God grant me the wisdom and courage to change the things I cannot accept."
Amy Serrano

"We become so focused on the work of the Lord that we forget the Lord of the work."
Oscar Serrano

ANSWERING COMPASSION'S CALL

A Story of God's Call to Help Those in Desperate Need

AMY SERRANO

"Pure religion and undefiled before God and the Father is this, To visit the fatherless and widows in their affliction, and to keep himself unspotted from the world." (James 1:27)

Answering Compassion's Call

Worldwide Heart to Heart Ministries is a charity organized under section 501(c)(3) of the Internal Revenue Code in the US and is a nonprofit organization registered as ASOCORA in Honduras.

Cover Design: Sarah Serrano

Answering Compassion's Call is a memoir written by Amy Serrano which documents her recollections of people, places and events in her life and ministry. It is possible that your recollections differ from those of Amy. However, the purpose of this book is to document Amy's recollections.

Answering Compassion's Call / Amy Serrano –First Edition

ISBN 978-1-7354067-2-5 (Paperback)
ISBN 978-1-7354067-0-1 (e-Book Printable PDF)
ISBN 978-1-7354067-3-2 (e-Book Slide Reader PDF)

Published by Worldwide Heart to Heart Ministries
PO Box 3275
Clackamas, OR 97015 USA

Dedication

To My Heroes…

The amazing, resilient children of Honduras. They have suffered much and are the forgotten ones. This book is written so that you know God did not forget you, and in fact, He has moved and will move heaven and earth for you. I also must remember my other heroes, all of those who have served on our board of directors, gone down to Honduras, dedicated time and money, sponsored our kids and prayed for us. This is your story! We have long wanted to write this story for you, so that you can see what your sacrifice has amounted to. Most of all we want to thank the God of the fatherless, Jesus Christ! He is the author of this ministry and this book and all glory be to Him. He saw the broken-hearted children and heard their prayers, and He has shown His greatness in the midst of great darkness.

My Prayer…

Lord, I pray for each person that reads this book that it may be a source of inspiration. Father, I pray that it will take them on a journey to Your Heart, and they would see that you have not forgotten your precious children. I pray for all of those who have stood beside us, worldwide, to accomplish all that has been done in these last twenty years. I pray that their blessings will be overflowing.

I pray for the nation of Honduras, that You would shine a light into the darkness. Breathe Your Spirit into the church, into the government and into the lives of each person. We especially pray for the children. They need a miracle today, and You are their Savior. Thy kingdom come and Thy will be done, in Honduras, as it is in Heaven.

In Jesus name I pray, Amen.

Contents

Foreword

A life that blesses others goes on forever.

Amy Marie Serrano, beloved wife of Oscar Serrano, beloved mother of Sarah and Rachel, beloved spiritual mother of over 130 children who call her Mami, and author of this book, went home to be with Jesus suddenly, on Wednesday, December 26th, 2018. She was born, the fourth child of I.H. and Jackie Marie Rills on July 21, 1975. She is survived by the absolute love of her life, next to Jesus, Oscar B. Serrano, her husband of 22 years, her beloved beautiful daughters, Sarah and Rachel, all her spiritual children and family here in Honduras, her sister Connie and brother Ken, her Nana Callie, and all of her birth family in Louisiana. She was preceded in death by her mother, Jackie Marie Rills, her father, I.H. Rills, her brother Mark Rills, and her spiritual daughters Amabilia Ramos and Diana Posadas.

For years people told us we needed to write the amazing story of Worldwide Heart to Heart (H2H) to share with others how God uses His servants to accomplish His plans of compassion, if they are willing and obedient.

A few years ago, Amy got sick. She was bedridden for several days with a fever and the flu. When I went to see how she was doing, there she was, writing our story. She said, "Since I cannot get out of this bed to help, I may as well get something done!" And indeed, she did! Whenever she had a few minutes over the next several years, she added to the book.

The last entry was made in 2015.

Amy was the spiritual head of this ministry. She came up with the name Worldwide Heart to Heart, and God gave her our guiding scripture.

> *"Blessed be God, even the Father of our Lord Jesus Christ, the Father of mercies, and the God of all comfort; who comforteth us in all our tribulation, that we may be able to comfort them which are in any trouble, by the comfort wherewith we ourselves are comforted of God. For as the sufferings of Christ abound in us, so our consolation also aboundeth by Christ."*
> *(2 Corinthians 1:3-5)*

I remember the day in 2003 when Amy, Oscar, Sarah, Rachel, and Oscar's mom Eugenia, loaded up the car and trailer in Washington State, and headed for Honduras to live full time. Her last words to me were, "Mary, right now we need to begin looking for people to replace us in H2H, in case something happens to us." Imagine that! Well, we do not have anyone who will ever replace you, my beloved Amy. But I know God will bring the people He needs, as He has always done, to accomplish this work of His called Heart to Heart.

I *loved* listening to her pray. She could go so deep, to the root cause of needs and challenges for all of us, and with her words would conduct surgical prayer to cover them.

She taught me so much. Though I am thirty-two years older than Amy, she was my teacher, my hero, my wise counselor, and my best friend for the last twenty-one years. As we developed this ministry, we would all talk about how to do things and what plans needed to happen. Amy would sit quietly through our discussion and when we were done, she would gently say, "Have you thought about this?" and proceed to lay out her thoughts, which were always right on the nose.

Her wisdom was beyond her years, and I know it came straight from the mind of Christ, because she stayed intimately close to Him.

One day Amy and I were discussing the Prayer of Serenity which says, "God grant me the serenity to accept the things I cannot change; courage to change the things I can; and the wisdom to know the difference."

Amy replied emphatically, "That's not *my* prayer! Mine is, 'God grant me the wisdom and courage to change the things I cannot accept.'" That is Amy's philosophy in a nutshell.

In early 2017, God told Amy that whenever a team came to Honduras and she was teaching the Sunday School lesson for the "gringos", she was to give her testimony. From then on, she always did just that. I have heard her testimony more times than I can count, and I must honestly say, I never tired of hearing it. In fact, each time, it brought me to tears, and to a closer walk with Jesus. So, here it is, what I know she wants you to hear, and in her own words.

Mary Frenter
President, Worldwide Heart to Heart

Amy Serrano and her sibling in Louisiana

Siblings reunited in Louisiana. Connie Pearce, Amy Serrano, Ken Rills, Mark Rills

Introduction

"And as for thy nativity, in the day thou wast born thy navel was not cut, neither wast thou washed in water to supple thee; thou wast not salted at all, nor swaddled at all. None eye pitied thee, to do any of these unto thee, to have compassion upon thee; but thou wast cast out in the open field, to the loathing of thy person, in the day that thou wast born. And when I passed by thee, and saw thee polluted in thine own blood, I said unto thee when thou wast in thy blood, Live; yea, I said unto thee when thou wast in thy blood, Live."
(Ezekiel 16:4-6)

What a sad story told here in the Old Testament book of Ezekiel! It is the bitter story of abandonment. Verses four and five tell of an unspeakable injustice: the abandonment of an innocent child. However, it does not end there…but God! You will see me mention that phrase many times in this book, because it speaks of an evil, an injustice, or darkness too ugly for restoration, too big for solving, and too far beyond our reach…but God!

What is the real beauty of this story? It is that this is our story, the human story, my story. We were all unlovely at one time. But God passed by and saw us, and saved us, and washed us, and made us beautiful. In the time that I most needed a savior, God saw me, and gave me a home and a family in Him. The beauty is that He still saves and still runs to the lost, the abused, and the despised. And He shows us this compassion, so that we can bring that compassion to others.

The ministry's guiding scripture is:

> *"Blessed be God, even the Father of our Lord Jesus Christ, the Father of mercies, and the God of all comfort; who comforteth us in all our tribulation, that we may be able to comfort them which are in any trouble, by the comfort wherewith we ourselves are comforted of God. For as the sufferings of Christ abound in us, so our consolation also aboundeth by Christ."*
> *(2 Corinthians 1:3-5)*

Once God has brought us through, we then have something to give, and there are those who need what we have. It is the gift of compassion. May God lead us to those who need compassion today.

1

Oscar's Story

"Then thou spakest in vision to thy holy one, and saidst, I have laid help upon one that is mighty; I have exalted one chosen out of the people." (Psalm 89:19)

Like David before him, Oscar was surely called to be God's servant to His children in Honduras. Psalm 89 goes on to say, "I have found...my servant; with my sacred oil I have anointed him. My hand will sustain him; surely my arm will strengthen him...My faithful love will be with him forever."

Oscar was born and raised in Puerto Cortes, a city on the north coast of Honduras, where our current Honduran Heart to Heart (H2H) administrative office is located. When one lands in Honduras, the warm tropical air immediately fills your senses. The lush vegetation you see below, as the plane comes in for a landing, makes you certain that you are going to be on an episode of *Lost*. It is a paradise in many ways, but underneath lies a darker truth. Honduras is amazing; I have lived here full-time since 2003. The food is incredible; the Spanish is distinct from any other Central American country, and the culture is colorful and alive. But Honduras is the second poorest country in the western hemisphere (the first is Haiti), and this poverty begets many social woes.

Crime is high, because police are paid less than $300 a month to risk their lives every day. For this reason, many of them turn to making the big bucks through corruption. For many families, just putting food on the table is a challenge, and much of the population over the age of thirty is illiterate. Few laws, and desperation caused by poverty and hopelessness, make a toxic combination.

Most youths have only two choices: the young men become cement mixers and hole diggers, spending their lives in extremely hard labor, barely earning enough money to put a small bit of beans and rice on the table, or they join gangs and have cell phones, drive around in fancy trucks and wear nice clothes; the girls either marry a man many years older than they are, who may already have several other wives, and endure abuse, or they turn to gangs and prostitution and hang on the arm of the gang member who's driving the fancy car and wearing the nice clothes. Either way, since many youths are sent out into the streets by their parents to find work, they are lured to the dark side.

This is the hard reality of the nation where my husband grew up. Oscar loves his native country and is proud to be called a Honduran. However, from an early age, he had a keen sense of what was right and what was wrong. At seven years of age, he accepted Jesus Christ as his Lord and Savior. It was for that very reason that he had the ability to discern what was going on around him. For many Hondurans this is all that they know, and they accept it as "normal".

Oscar always knew that God wanted something better for Honduras. He always dreamed of being a missionary. From his youth, he looked for ways to live his life in a way that brought hope to the hopeless. As a youth in his church, he asked his pastor's permission to go out to the Garifuna villages along the coast, to work with the natives. His pastor at the time did not think Oscar was ready, but still his heart burned to get started somewhere.

At the age of eighteen, he left home for the capital city of Tegucigalpa, Honduras to attend seminary and become a pastor. After completing seminary, Oscar returned to Puerto Cortes and found work as a warehouse supervisor at the Coca Cola company, which had its offices right on the beach. Meanwhile, Oscar continued to keep his dream of doing something more for the Lord deep in his heart. He continued to hear the cry of his own people and prayed that the Lord would show him His will.

In 1994 Park West Children's fund, now known as "Friendships", based in Lake Charles, Louisiana, took a missionary voyage; its destination was Puerto Cortes, Honduras. It was a 300-foot cargo ship that went into ports around the world delivering goods that would be used by local churches and ministries. It was called the "Spirit Ship", or as I like to call it, "Oscar's ride to his destiny"! When Oscar heard that the ship was in the port, and that some locals were applying as missionaries, his heart leapt for joy. After a time of prayer, he felt certain that the Lord had told him that it would not pull out of Puerto Cortes without him.

Oscar, however, had some challenges. His father had passed away years before, and his mother was a single mom trying to raise Oscar's two younger siblings. When Oscar found work at the Coca Cola Company, he told his mother to retire, and that he would provide for her from then on. If he were to go on the ship, he could no longer keep that promise. So, Oscar decided in his heart that he would not go. His mother found out about what had happened and reprimanded him for his decision. She told Oscar that she did not want to be the reason that he did not fulfil his calling from God, and that she would go back to work.

Oscar went to the ship and applied, but to his great disappointment, he was immediately turned down. The captain told him that their crew was already at capacity and could no longer accept more staff. Oscar's heart sank, but he continued to pray, "Lord, I believe you told me I was to go; I'm just going to leave it up to you." The next day he really thought that his dreams were crushed. From his office window, he could see the entire port. And each day he would look out at the port and pray for the ship, its crew, and its mission in Honduras.

The ship sat in port for many weeks, and one morning, he saw it pulling out. He watched as the ship faded into the horizon and tears rolled down his cheeks. For hours he went sadly through his morning. When he could no longer contain his disappointment, he hid himself in the bathroom. He prayed to the Lord, "I was so sure that you wanted me to go on that ship, and now it's gone." He said he clearly heard the voice of the Lord telling him it was not over; he needed to keep believing.

Oscar decided to trust the Lord, not knowing what God had in mind. Then, that afternoon, he saw a glorious sight; the ship had returned and was pulling into port. He later found out the ship had merely gone out to high sea to dump its bilge. The next day, the captain sent the ship's pastor to Oscar's work to find him, telling him that the captain wanted to see Oscar immediately. Oscar hurried down to the ship, and the captain told him there had been a few crew changes, and they were now in need of some new staff. Oscar was hired immediately. Three weeks later, the ship set off for Galveston, Texas with Oscar Serrano on board.

Oscar spent two years on the Spirit Ship. In 1995, we met when I was sent from my job in the main office of Friendships in San Pedro, California, to work on the ship in Galveston. We married nearly a year later in September of 1996.

While we were on the ship, we met a family who hailed from the Pacific Northwest, Eric and Laura Smith and their two children, Jared and Alisha. They came on board the Spirit Ship to go on a short-term mission to the Caribbean. Eric worked in the engine room with Oscar, and Laura and I became great friends. When the ship returned to port, the Smiths returned to Washington State, and Oscar and I got married.

We left the ship in August of 1996 and began helping a small Hispanic church in the Texas City, Texas area. We lived with the pastor after we were married, and Oscar led worship for the church. I taught in their Sunday School. Oscar was now in the place where God began to move him into his life-long destiny.

Oscar, Fermin, Alex, and Victor in front of the Spirit ship

Vio and Oscar working inside the Spirit ship's engine room

Maria, Oscar, Peter, Leen, Halley

Oscar and friends from the ship

2

The Early Years

"For I know the thoughts that I think toward you, saith the Lord, thoughts of peace, and not of evil, to give you an expected end." (Jeremiah 29:11)

We stayed in contact with the Smiths, who repeatedly invited us to come and visit them in Washington. In November 1996, shortly after we had married, we headed from Houston, Texas, to Portland, Oregon, on a Greyhound bus. It took us four days to get there, but praise God, we arrived safe and sound. Our luggage had been lost, but that's another story.

We immediately fell in love with the Pacific Northwest. We loved its abundant greenery and cool climate; thank goodness we both love the rain! We stayed with the Smiths for two weeks and then returned to Texas, but we knew we wanted to go back and call Washington home. Eric had just opened a heating and air-conditioning business and told Oscar that he would have a job if he did come back. In February of 1997, we officially became Washingtonians.

We lived with the Smiths for the first few months, until we were able to get our own place. We joined a small Assemblies of God Church in the little town of Castle Rock, Washington, where we now lived. The community embraced us, and life began to move forward as normal. But Oscar continued to say to me, "Amy, if we are going to live here in the US and make good money, I don't just want to stand here and be comfortable, I want to do something for *my* country." His heart was burdened mostly for the children, the most helpless members of society. He told me that because of what he had seen growing up, and because of what he himself had lived through, he could not rest until something was done to make a change.

Oscar often talked to the Smiths and others in our church about his desire to do something. Most folks simply patted him on the back and said, "Well, God bless you. I hope God opens the doors." Some even told him, "That's not going to happen!" But he never gave up, and God would soon put the people in place who would begin to help create what Oscar had been dreaming all those years.

One day, as Oscar spoke with Eric's dad, Bob Smith, about what he wanted to do, Bob told him that he had some friends who were retired school teachers who were very organized Christian people who might be able to help him make a plan to get started. I don't know if you believe in divine appointments, but on that night, we met the two people who we have served side by side with since 1997.

Mary and Lyle Frenter had recently retired from teaching and were looking forward to traveling and developing their apartment rental business. But, in keeping with His nature, God knows what we really need. That night, Oscar explained to the Frenters all the beauties and horrors of Honduras. Mary sat cross-legged on a bed in their apartment's living room, and Lyle sat in his recliner.

We talked for hours as they listened raptly to the stories and smiled excitedly as Oscar expressed how he wanted to help. Mary took notes in a tablet, and the two generously shared all their knowledge and ideas on organization. For the first time, we were not hearing the question *why*, but rather, *why not*. The couple agreed to help us get started, and we made a plan that night. The first step was to become registered as a 501c3 nonprofit organization in the state of Washington.

Later, we sat with the Smiths and their brother Paul, coming up with potential names for our new organization. After numerous ideas were tossed around, we settled on "Haven of Refuge". The next day Laura and I drove up to Olympia, Washington to legally register as a nonprofit organization. In early 1997 we got to work.

Our first act as a nonprofit was to send a container on a cargo ship to Vietnam. Paul Smith had visited Vietnam with another organization and had friends and connections that he wanted to help. St. John's Hospital of Longview, Washington, had donated a large number of medical items that we loaded first. Most of the other things we put in the container were junk. Much of the donated clothing was unusable and the project required a massive amount of sorting and cleaning. In the end, the container was sent.

In the meantime, we met with the Frenters to plan an investigative trip to Honduras. The idea was to see what doors God would open and what God wanted us to do. In January of 1998, Paul Smith, Oscar, and I traveled to Honduras.

It was an exciting trip for me. I had never met my mother-in-law. I was four months pregnant with our first child, and I was thrilled to be there. Walking off the airplane onto the tarmac, I remember feeling almost slapped in the face by the stifling heat and humidity and being big and pregnant didn't help that feeling. All the same, the trip was magical. I met my husband's family and for the first time experienced the wonderful culture of the country I now call home.

That trip to Honduras changed me forever. It was one of the steps God took in answering my "dangerous" prayer. I was introduced to situations that broke my heart and brought me up close and personal to the desperate need in our world in a way I never had experienced before. As our plane took off for Washington, tears rolled down my cheeks, and I silently vowed to the land I was leaving that I would return.

Amy and Oscar's wedding day, Texas City, Texas in
Miembros Iglesia -1996

Laura Smith, Robert,
Paul, Diana Smith
Family

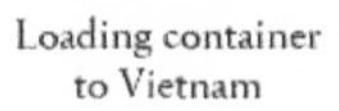

Loading container
to Vietnam

Eric and Laura Smith

Laura Smith

Amy and Diana

Eric and Laura Smith, Oscar, Paul and Diana

3
Amy's Story

"Brethren, I count not myself to have apprehended: but this one thing I do, forgetting those things which are behind, and reaching forth unto those things which are before, I press toward the mark for the prize of the high calling of God in Christ Jesus." (Philippians 3:13-14)

To be honest, I am the most shocked of all that I ended up part of this great work of God. The truth is, until now, I had never succeeded at anything. All my friends in high school knew me as a clown who just didn't care. I was the jokester, but underneath it all I had died inside. My mom passed away when I was nine years old. From that point on, I knew what it meant to lose all hope. My dad remarried some years later to a woman who suffered from severe mental illness. The next four years of my life were filled with physical and emotional abuse. By the time I was fourteen, I had lost all hope and the desire to live. Because I did not have a strong sense of self, I came to believe what my stepmother often told me, that I was the one who killed my mother with my selfishness.

I was born late in my mother's life; she was forty years old. But according to my dad, I was not an accident. My mother always wanted a big family. However, nine years had gone by in their marriage and my mother could not become pregnant. She prayed to God and began a series of treatments with her doctor. My mother often suffered from irregular and painful periods. Her doctor finally told her, "Jackie you are sterile. Why don't you just get a hysterectomy and be done with it?" My mother sadly agreed, and the doctor planned the surgery. My mom told her sister, my aunt Callie, about her plans to have a hysterectomy. My aunt wisely advised her, "Jackie why don't you just go to a doctor who you don't know and get a second opinion?" My mother took my aunt's advice, and to her great shock, she was three months pregnant with my sister!

So, as she was nine years behind on her great dream of having a big family, she had children clear until she couldn't any longer. My mother had other physical problems as well. She had a severe heart murmur and asthma. My mom died at forty-eight of a massive heart attack. Her death was almost instant. For years, I heard how her death was caused by me. First, because she was too sick and old to be having children at her age, and second, because I was a selfish brat, who sucked all the life out of her. Once, I remember a school counselor asking me about my mom, and I told her that I had killed my mother. She replied, "But I thought you said she died of a heart attack." I replied, "Oh, yes, she did, but I'm the reason for that." The counselor said nothing to me, other than agreeing with me that it was probably my fault.

I don't exactly remember the last straw. I remember I had a fight with a friend, practically my only friend, and I had reached the bottom. I remember being in science class days before, where the science teacher had told us that the best way to commit suicide was to take aspirin. My parents were at work. I only remember finding a small bottle of aspirin and lots of other pills, and to this day, I don't know what they were. I remember swallowing, frantically. Even today, I can hardly take pills without my gag reflex starting, remembering taking all those chalky pills, mouthfuls at a time, chewing them up and swallowing.

After frantically downing every pill in my parent's medicine cabinet, I went and lay down on my bed and waited to die. I believed in God. I was raised Catholic and was taught about His reality. I was taught many stories in the Bible and honestly believed that God was good, but I believed even more so, that I was not. I can remember lying in bed and asking God to take me away from there and closed my eyes. I didn't die. I fell asleep. I remember waking up slightly disappointed, but thought, "Well that figures, I can't even kill myself right!"

I got up and went to make dinner. By that time, my parents had come home from work. I ate dinner, did the dishes and went off to my room to start my homework. I don't remember anything until I woke up the next day in the hospital. My dad said that he called me to bring out a detention slip he had to sign, and I never answered. He went to my room to try and find me and did not see me. But just as he was about to close the door, he saw the nightstand on the other side of my bed begin to shake. He walked around the bed to find me having a seizure on the floor.

I spent a few days in the hospital and then a month in a rehab center, where everyone sat around and asked why in the world I would want to do something like that. My dad however, realized that he and my stepmother needed to separate. They did, and my dad moved us back to the town where I was born. Over time, life became much more bearable. But it was also in the next few years that I began the spiritual voyage that would take me through everything from devil worship to new age. I loved all things about the occult and witchcraft. They made me less powerless. But in all my searching and wondering, I kept coming back to the faith that I had been raised in, the Christian faith. For some reason, Jesus Christ had always had a powerful fascination for me. Each time I looked away, I knew I was looking away from the truth.

I eventually wound up in a drug rehab facility with a counselor who was a born-again Christian. I remember that I really enjoyed my conversations with her about God and spirituality. I felt that I was being fed some powerful truth. I began to pray each night before I went to sleep. I would look out of my window and begin to speak with God. Within the next few months, I gave my heart to Jesus and started attending church. I got baptized in the Holy Spirit and started to have strange desires to live my life just for Jesus. One day while I was in church, the pastor addressed the youth and said, "Who knows, maybe some of you will end up missionaries in China." A very definite voice came into my head saying, "You're one of them." I didn't really get that it was China exactly, but I knew it would be the mission field for sure.

We had a visiting pastor come for a special service at our church. He called forward all the youth who wanted to go to the mission field. All the pastors' and deacons' children went forward, and I felt certain that I did not deserve to stand among them. So, I simply sat at my seat and said, "Lord, here I am. Send me!" Perhaps I could scrub the toilets for these great men and woman of God. Little did I know that within months of that time, I would be heading out to be a missionary and would never come back home.

The town that I grew up in was about thirty minutes southwest of Baton Rouge, Louisiana, which is where the church I attended was located, but we had cell groups in our own town. About six months after I became a Christian and started attending the church, the ministry, Park West Children's Fund, later known as "Friendships", came to the port of Baton Rouge, and the ministry joined forces with our church. The cell groups in the church "adopted" missionaries on the ship and attended to them in the best ways they could by taking them to the dentist, to the eye doctor, to the movies, and to visit in our homes. It was in these meetings with missionaries from Guatemala, that I knew I was supposed to be on that ship.

One night after coming back from a dinner at one of those cell groups, I told my parents, my dad had again remarried, "Guess what? I'm going to be a missionary on a ship, isn't that great?" "Oh, wonderful, sweetheart," my dad said, barely acknowledging me, as he read through the newspaper. But I knew. I sent my application in and waited for their response.

When my parents understood that I was serious about this, they were strongly opposed. My dad thought that I needed to get my life established first, before I tried something like this. I made my mind up, that if God really wanted me to go, I would obey them and would let Him change their hearts. I had sent in my application and was praying my parents' change of heart would be my confirmation that it was God's will for me to go.

I remember the day that the letter came in the mail. It said, "Dear Amy Rills, we would love to have you come and be part of our ministry at our main offices in San Pedro, California." I don't remember too many other times that I have felt so joyful! But I still had the little issue of my parents' blessing. I had already made a promise to God that I would obey them and that would be my sign that it was His will for me to go. I remember the night that I brought the letter to show them. I was so nervous. I did not know what their response was going to be.

I pulled the letter out of the envelope and said, "Well, I've been accepted to that ship I told you about." My stepmom leaped out of her seat with excitement. To my astonishment, my dad also smiled and said, "Wow, that is wonderful!" "What? I thought you said I shouldn't go! I thought you were against this! Why the change of heart?" My dad told me that he was never really against it but did not think that they would accept me because I was so young. He did not want my heart broken over it. But now that they were going to accept me, my parents were elated and even agreed to pay for my ticket to California!

However, I had another challenge. My spiritual leader, who was my cell group leader, also thought it might not be a good idea for me to go. Once I got my acceptance letter, I brought it to her, as well. She read it over and said, "Well, why don't we just go and talk to the pastor about this?" The next Sunday, we met with our pastor after service. I sat to one side, as I watched my cell leader and pastor read through the letter together. They discussed it some, the pastor had a warm smile on his face, and then they called me over. My Pastor said he was very excited and so happy that I would be going, and that he felt that this was God's will for me. Two weeks later, I was on a plane to Los Angeles.

I spent three wonderful years on the ship and married my awesome husband. However, I need to go back and tell you about my "dangerous" prayer.

As I mentioned, I was serving in the ship ministry, but really did not understand why. I believed I was a compassionate person, but I could not understand poverty. I was raised to believe in hard work and pulling your own weight. I did not understand that places existed in the world were a man could work fourteen-hour days of hard labor and still not make enough to feed his family. My eyes were blind, and I knew it. So, I simply prayed and asked the Lord to open them. It took Him about five years to do it, but once they were opened everything changed.

I remember it was about two to three days after I had prayed that prayer. I was in the dining hall on the ship. There were some Christian magazines on the coffee table that I began to thumb through. It was 1994. Do any of you remember the headlines from that year? Let me refresh your memory: they were all about Rwanda. The magazine had a four- or five-page article about the travesties that were going on at the time, but one part of the article uprooted me.

It was a picture of a young boy with no legs on a skateboard with a man standing over him beating him with a belt. The caption below the picture said that the child had not been born without legs; they had been amputated because he was an orphan, in order to make him a better beggar. I am sure that by amputations, they meant by machete! What's more, they said that the man standing over him was his pimp. He was being beaten, because he had not come up with his quota from begging that day. The worst case of holy anger rose up in me. The injustice was more than I could bear. Where was their CPS in all of this? I was completely clueless. But it was at that point, I started to "get it", that beyond my safe, clean world, was a world that was broken, unfair and crying out for help because they were helpless.

Life went on. I married and had the chance to go to Honduras for my first time with my husband in 1998. As I mentioned before, the trip was amazing and troubling at the same time. While on that trip, some friends took us out to the local garbage dump. You knew that you were getting close because of the horrible smell. When we arrived, the scene that greeted us was a large landfill area with huge piles of stinking garbage. Children were crawling all over the piles like ants. I wish I could tell you that they were older kids; however, they were babies, all about five years old and younger.

We found one little boy about eight years old and began to talk to him about how his life was. He told us all that he wanted to do was go to school. I looked around as tiny little people scavenged through the garbage for anything that they could find to eat, to keep, or to sell. They had partially eaten tortillas that they had found in the garbage, drying out on rocks to eat. They were fighting off vultures with seven-foot wing spans.

I remember someone said, "Get in the taxi. There's a drunk coming!" I saw across the field a man who looked about 200 years old walking toward us, with nothing on but his birthday suit. They grabbed me and threw me into the car and quickly drove away. I struggled to look out the back window as this man made his way to the children who stood helplessly as the man approached. I thought, no, this is not right; get the kids out of there.

On that same trip, we also went to see the public hospital. Now you must understand, I was pregnant at the time and the hospital was very scary. The whole place was covered in rust and the mattresses had blood stains on them. We came to a certain area where they had supposedly sterile gloves washed out and hung to dry. One of the most difficult places to visit was the children's ward. There were a few kids there when we went up. One was a sick, little girl who was there with her mother.

In that same room there was also a little girl who was all alone. She was about two years old and was burning up with fever but was not crying. In the public hospital, they offer you a hospital bed and nothing more. You must bring your own sheets, pillow, water, fans as there is no air conditioning, toilet paper and just about everything you might need during your hospital stay. This little girl was just sitting on the bare, plastic mattress. We were told that her mother brought her in but left her there because she had to work. The little girl was in a very soiled cloth diaper and just sat there with her eyes fixed on the other little girl and her mother taking care of her.

I was young and scared and didn't know very much about babies, but I wanted to hold her and care for her so badly. Unfortunately, I didn't. I was too scared to touch her. I laugh, because had that been me now, I would have taken charge of the situation, "Get me a diaper. Let's go buy her some food. I'll sit with her until her mother comes back," but no, at that time I had no idea what to do.

You could see in her eyes the desperation and need, as she watched all the other children being cared for. Then it happened, the levy broke! She began to cry a cry that came from her soul. Her wailing could be heard throughout the hospital. She was screaming for the attention that she so desperately needed. At that point, I cowered even more, and we left.

A few years later Oscar was pastoring a church in Washington State, and I was big and pregnant with our second child, Rachel. We were at the church, and it was late, and I was tired. Oscar was in a meeting with the church leadership, while I stayed out in the sanctuary caring for all the kids. I watched my one-and-a-half-year-old daughter Sarah running around playing, and all of a sudden I started to think of the children out at the dump and wondered what they were going to eat tonight, and where they were going to sleep. The thought came to my mind of my Sarah being there wandering around until she found a safe place to hide and sleep.

I can't even describe the extreme sadness that came over me. It was the worst feeling of sadness I had felt in all of my life. I ran into the bathroom and began to cry so hard that I fell to the ground. I worried because the kids were out there alone. The leaders would soon be coming out of the meeting and were going to think that something was wrong with me. I prayed, "Oh God, help me get it together, so that I don't scare anyone." I stayed in the bathroom for five more minutes, washed my face and got my composure back. The meeting ended, and we headed back home.

That night we had some missionary friends from Guatemala staying at our house, and Oscar stayed up late talking with them. It was late, about 11:00 pm, as I headed to bed. Just as soon as I lay my head down, I began to think about the little girl in the hospital bed and started thinking, "What if that was Sarah in that hospital bed?" Again, this deep sadness came over me, this time worse than before. I went into the bathroom and sobbed, uncontrollably.

The sadness was so bad that I almost thought it was demonic and began to cast it away. It was then that I felt God speak to me and say, "No, Amy, it's not the devil. Twice today, I let you see what I see." You see, those are His children, and His heart is broken! He used my child to help me see that those are His children. I sat and cried for at least 30 minutes on my bathroom floor.

The prayer that I had prayed nearly five years earlier, had been answered and there was no going back. I can remember thinking, "So this is what reality is, Lord? This is the truth, dark and hopeless?" I sat on my floor thinking, "It's all messed up, no hope at all."

Suddenly something rose up in me. I got up off the floor and looked at myself in the mirror, "What you are doing on the floor?" I said to myself, "Wash your face; you have work to do." I decided that day that I was no longer going to cry about it. I was going to do something about it. For me personally, H2H started that day. When the dark realities and gross injustices are put in my face, I just say, "Okay Lord, we just need to fight harder!" And that is what I have done ever since.

Spirit Ship that
Amy & Oscar served on

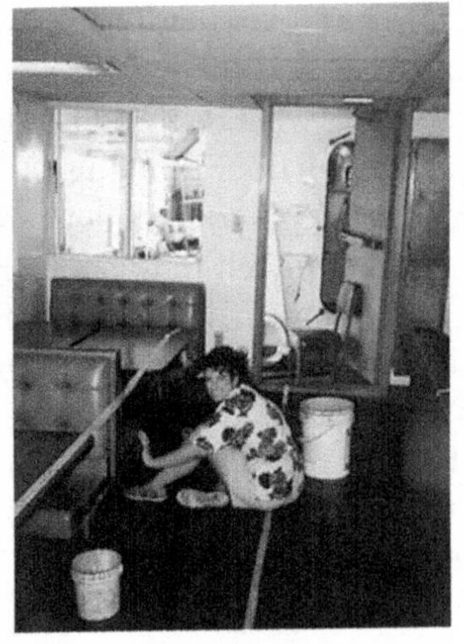

Amy cleaning the
dining area

Members of the
Spirit ship

"El Basurero" (garbage dump) in Puerto Cortes, Cortes, Honduras in 1998

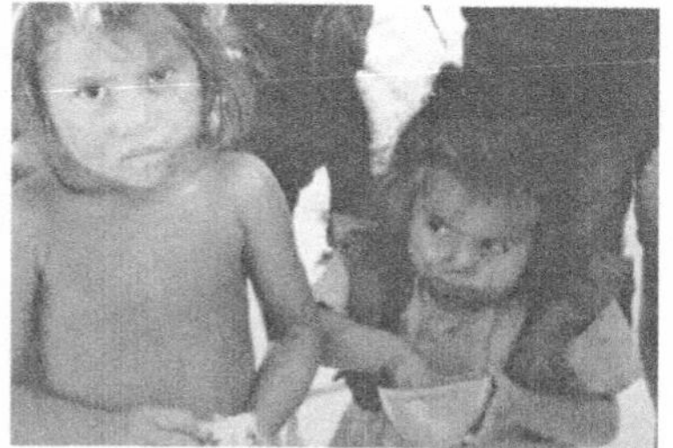

Kids living at the garbage dump and looking for food

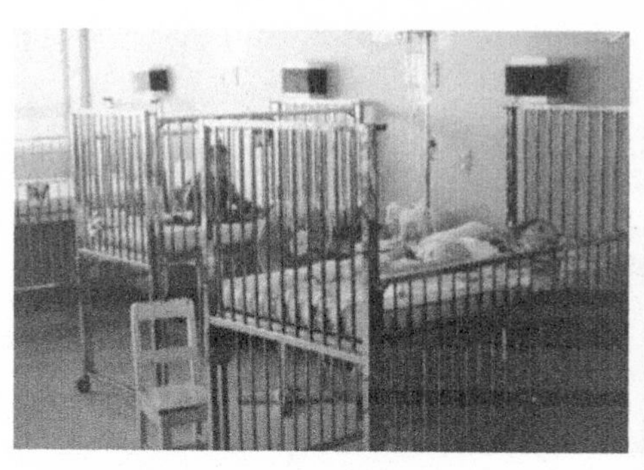

Babies in a hospital in Puerto Cortes, Honduras - 1998

4

Becoming Worldwide Heart to Heart Ministries

"Be strong and of a good courage, fear not, nor be afraid of them: for the Lord thy God, he it is that doth go with thee; he will not fail thee, nor forsake thee." (Deuteronomy 31:6)

After that first trip I went on to Honduras, we came back to the United States and presented what we had seen to our church. At that point, things began to unravel for us. I became terribly ill on the flight back and ended up staying three days in the hospital. The Smiths closed their business due to a back-injury Eric had sustained years before in a logging accident. Oscar found work in Spokane, but that was eight hours away from where we were currently living in Castle Rock, Washington. The ministry ground to a halt.

I was still living with our new-born baby girl Sarah in the Castle Rock area. We were beginning to make plans to move permanently to Spokane, but we could never get away from the thing that the Lord was burdening our hearts to do. Oscar was offered a very lucrative job in Spokane, but after a time of prayer, we decided to turn it down. We wanted to stay in western Washington where we believed God would develop the ministry.

It was then, in 1998, that disaster hit Honduras. It was October 29th, the peak of hurricane season in the western Caribbean. The last major hurricane to take aim at Honduras was Hurricane Fifi, a category three hurricane that struck Omoa in 1974. Fifi caused major destruction on the northwestern coast. Now, something far worse was bearing down upon Honduras, and its name was Hurricane Mitch.

One of only five category-five hurricanes to make landfall in recorded history in the Americas, Hurricane Mitch went down in history as one of the deadliest natural disasters to ever strike Latin America. I remember watching the news each day, as the threat grew more and more imminent for Honduras. I spoke with my husband on the phone, and he told me not to worry because normally the storms pass to the north. This time that would not be the case. Hurricane Mitch hit Honduras straight on as a category five hurricane; and it hit Honduras in the most devastating way that Honduras can be hit.

In Honduras, the biggest danger that a storm can pose is not wind, but rain. Honduras has an extremely mountainous topography, and in late October, the middle of the rainy season, with already saturated ground, the last thing anyone wants is a dramatic amount of rain. Hurricane Mitch moved in over the country and then stalled there. The rainfall reached a rate of about four inches per hour, with total rainfall exceeding thirty inches along the coast and fifty inches in the country's interior. The country was ravaged.

Our church was deeply concerned for Oscar's family who were all in the Puerto Cortes area and wanted to know what they could do to help. Some asked if they could send something, and then began calling us to see if their friends and family could send things as well. Oscar got in touch with his former pastor in Honduras and asked him if they could work together on getting a shipment to the folks in need. His pastor was more than ready to be of service. Then we got the news that a local Washington hospital was donating medical equipment. So, what was initially just a few items to go to Oscar's family, turned into enough goods to fill a forty-foot container.

By that time our ministry "Haven of Refuge" had disbanded, and we were now working under the legal and spiritual covering of our church. Many local pastors and church members helped us pack the container and got it ready to go. At the same time, our pastors,

Roy and Linda Henson, thought that it would be a good idea for us to be in Honduras to receive the container. In March of 1999, Oscar and I and our ten-month old baby Sarah were sent to Honduras for one month. For additional help, we brought along David, a young man Oscar had met while working in Spokane. While we were there, we stayed in the home of a friend of Oscar's.

When Oscar went to the port authorities to arrange to receive our container, he was told by the dock master that if we sent the container, they would not accept it. The Honduran infrastructure was in absolute shambles. Without roads or bridges it would be impossible to get the items to rural areas. It was a logistical nightmare, compounded by the fact that many do-gooders from around the world had sent containers of goods to Honduras with no consignee to receive them. Eight hundred containers were stranded at the Port of Cortes. The dock master told Oscar that if he really wanted to help, he should take one of the containers that didn't have an owner and get it out of there. So, we called back to the United State and told them not to send the container.

At that time, Dole Food Company, Inc. was shipping humanitarian supplies to Honduras for free from a port in Texas, so we had raised enough funds to ship our container to Texas. Since we no longer needed those funds for shipping our container, we were able to use the money to make the first payment on a used pickup truck. With that truck, we secured one of the containers stranded on the dock and began taking the supplies where they were needed most.

Oscar and our friend Marcel and his family, went out each day, taking the goods up into the mountains and remote villages. One day, they came upon a boys' orphanage in the remote village of La Pita. The home was run by a local church and housed thirty boys. It was a beautiful property with a decent building that had nice bunks for all the boys, but that was where the attention ended. The boys were cared for by an eighteen-year old young man, who was basically just a boy himself. There was no income to support this institution, so the boys fished and begged on the streets in order to eat. We were told by the church overseeing the project that some

Americans had come, built the building, promised all kinds of help and then abandoned the kids.

We were mortified. When Oscar spoke with the people from the church in charge of this boys' home, he asked in what ways, other than simply funding the living expenses for the kids, could we be of help. The pastor told Oscar that what the boys really needed was a hope and a future. He suggested developing and building a technical training school, so that the boys could learn marketable skills.

Upon returning to the United States, we presented a video we had filmed while in Honduras detailing what we had seen to our church. It vividly portrayed the situation that these boys were in. Our church was not large or wealthy, but every member was moved to tears as they watched the poor-quality home videos we had made of the boys' home. In one day, enough people had stepped forward that we were able to sponsor the living expenses of all those boys at $30 a month each.

At that point, we knew we were ready to reorganize as a ministry. Mary and Lyle Frenter enthusiastically took charge of all the sponsors for the boys. Pastor Roy and Linda Henson also came along side us to help establish this budding vision. It was agreed that we needed to restructure as a ministry with our own identity as a 501c3 non-profit in Washington State. In the fall of 1999, Pastor Roy became the new president, resigning as pastor of our church to become the head of our board of directors for the fledgling ministry. A new name was voted on, and in April 2000, we officially became known as Worldwide Heart to Heart Ministries (H2H).

The Pita's Orphanage back in March 1998

Pastor Roy and Linda Henson in Honduras

Sarah's first Birthday. June 30th, 1999

5

Divine Appointments

"Since thou wast precious in my sight, thou hast been honourable, and I have loved thee: therefore will I give men for thee, and people for thy life." (Isaiah 43:4)

Meanwhile, we formed a new governing board that consisted of the Frenters, the Hensons, the Serranos, and Karl Germunson, a member of our church. In the fall of 1999, word began spreading to local churches and neighbors that a January 2000 mission trip to Honduras was in the works. The plan was to build a technical school to train the boys living at the orphanage H2H was supporting in La Pita, Honduras.

During this time, Mary was on one of her daily walks through Castle Rock, when she noticed a new medical clinic opening. She decided to go in and welcome them to the community. As soon as she entered the clinic, she met Dr. Anwar Ayoub, who had studied medicine in Spain and spoke fluent Spanish. Mary encouraged him to come to Honduras. She shared that we had recently started working with a children's home in La Pita, and that they could use medical care. Dr. Ayoub immediately lit up with joy, as he said it had been his hope for many years to work in a Central American country.

In addition, Castle Rock Christian Church's Pastor Ed Miller had recently held an evangelical crusade in India and asked us about the possibility of doing one in Honduras. Over a three-month period from January to March of 2000, fifty-one people headed to Honduras on various teams for what was a medical, evangelical, and construction frenzy! We were young and inexperienced at the time, but by the grace of God it all worked out. During the days, construction crews worked on the building project, and medical teams were taken up into the mountains to serve remote villages that seldom receive such care. Each night an evangelical crusade was held back in Puerto Cortes. Unfortunately, I couldn't be a part of any of those teams. I was at home giving birth to our second child, Rachel, who was born in February. But I knew our work in Honduras was just beginning.

Those were our first real teams, and we knew it was the start of something glorious. We continued to work with the boys' home, faithfully sending funds to feed, clothe, and educate them. However, we began receiving disturbing reports about conditions at the home. Our friends who delivered the funds and supplies to the boys, reported that the conditions in the home had not improved. They told us that many of the boys were still not in school and were living off the streets. One of the early mission teams had purchased pots, pans, plates, cups, utensils, and many other items to run the home. Our friends told us that they could no longer find any of those things. We were bitterly disappointed.

Another of our friends told us he had spoken to a local man in Puerto Cortes who told us we needed to find and talk to the gentlemen who had come from the United States to build the orphanage. This local man told us he did not know the whole story but knew that the builder had left town very angry after he argued with the pastor in charge of the orphanage.

In April, we finally found the gentleman who had built the orphanage building. He was a retired executive from the John Deere Corporation and lived in Tennessee. He told us that he had come to Honduras to help and had been cheated by that church. All the funds he had been sending down for the boys' home had been misappropriated by the church. This directly contradicted the story we had received from the pastor who had told us the builder had abandoned them. Our board decided we needed to go ourselves to see firsthand what was happening. In September of 2000, the Frenters, the Hensons, and Oscar headed to Honduras.

As soon as they entered the orphanage, Oscar found the situation was just as reported. When they opened the refrigerator there was no food and none of the boys were in school. All the equipment we had provided for the home was gone. It was immediately decided that H2H could no longer support this mission. Our hearts were broken. What would happen to those boys? The team fervently prayed for God to show us what we needed to do. This led to the first of many miracles that would happen on this incredible journey.

As was the custom in those early days, our team brought some wheelchairs down for anyone in need. When the local politicians found out about that, they made sure that it turned into a photo-op for themselves. The news cameras were called in, and as we handed the wheelchairs to some needy families, the mayor of Puerto Cortes had us shake his hand on television. While meeting with the mayor, we expressed to him our reason for being in Honduras. Because of the devastation wreaked by Hurricane Mitch, many kids were homeless and poverty stricken. We were there for those kids. After our talk, he told us that there was a man he wanted our team to meet. He said that this man was very wealthy and generous, and that he liked to help charities. He told us he would set up a meeting for that weekend.

On Sunday, the team drove on practically impassable roads out to this man's farm, about an hour outside of Puerto Cortes. They were greeted by a very humble looking man who could pass as a body double for Danny DeVito. That man was Salomon Lopez, the owner of the General Electric franchise in Honduras. He sat down next to Oscar and said, "I had a dream last night that you were coming, and God told me that I was to help you". He told them that he had a piece of property, not far away, that he wanted them to see. If we wanted it, it was ours.

They drove out to an eight-acre property right at the foot of the Merendón Mountain Range. It was the most beautiful piece of farmland any of them had ever seen. It was also the first time they had come face to face with angry cows! As they walked out onto the property, the current residents were not so pleased with their arrival. They were promptly chased away by 2000-pound "killer" cows. The hard reality was that this property was miles from civilization and could only reached by a rugged, rural road that required fording several rivers. But the board didn't care. When they looked out across this amazing piece of land, they envisioned a beautiful, new home for many homeless children. To them it was perfect.

The team returned to the United States elated. The future was clear. All our energies would now be spent on building a children's home on our wonderful new property. It was at this time we met two new people who would become part of our team and who would help us forge ahead with this vision. Curt and Phyllis Haas were members of our church. Curt was the owner of a construction company and Pastor Roy approached him about becoming involved with this endeavor. Rex and Cathy Rogers, also members of our church, were brought on board. Cathy, a nurse, and Rex, an electrician, were on our first team down to Honduras in January of 2000, and they desired to continue to help us with future teams.

For the first time, we sat down with our growing board and seriously discussed what we would do with the new property. While meeting at a local Castle Rock restaurant, the first plans of the future children's home were sketched out on a napkin by Linda Henson. Funds were soon raised and building began.

Now, more people were becoming aware of who we were and began signing up to go to Honduras. We were taking a construction team about once every six months and medical teams usually came along as well. The medical teams continued to take doctors and nurses up into the remote villages which did not have medical facilities. Tina Campbell, a member of Pastor Ed's church, led many Vacation Bible School (VBS) teams to Honduras and was the chairperson for many annual fundraising banquets back in the United States.

Any of the old alumni of those first H2H teams could tell you, it wasn't easy back in those days. We stayed in some "interesting" lodging with only aged vehicles for transportation. The road out to

Tegucigalpita, the tiny village which was the location of our new piece of property, was a rough one. There were many times we practically needed a hover craft to get out there. But those who came formed a special bond with this ministry, and many of them still come to Honduras and support the ministry as it continues to grow to face the ever-changing needs in Honduras.

Construction Team from Castle Rock in Tegucigalpita. February 19th, 2001

Linda Henson, Geri Sherwin, Kathi Rogers, Jean Costello and Phyllis Haas

Construction Team from Castle Rock, Washington and Workers from Honduras building the children's village in Tegucigalpita in 2003

Medical and dental team in Honduras - 2004

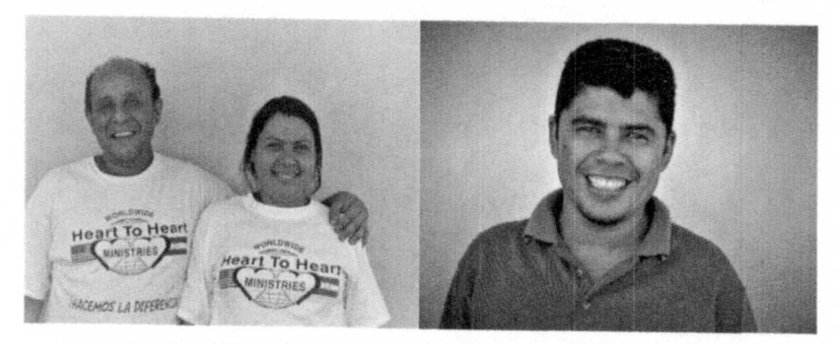

Marcel and Elvia Almendarez, and Freddy Castro who help the ministry.

6

The Waiting Is the Hardest Part

"For the vision is yet for an appointed time, but at the end it shall speak, and not lie: though it tarry, wait for it; because it will surely come, it will not tarry." (Habakkuk 2:3)

In 2000, Oscar found work at a local heating and air-conditioning company, but he distinctly felt God calling him to pastor a church again. Though Oscar had studied to be a pastor, his heart was not really in pastoring, but in mission work. For weeks he denied this call on his heart, but with each passing day, it got stronger.

He finally asked the Lord, "Okay, Lord, what do you want me to do?" God spoke to him and told him to go and see the Honduran pastor. "You mean the lying Honduran pastor?" he replied angrily. Several months before this, Oscar had met a Honduran man who pastored a small Hispanic church near our town. While talking with this man, Oscar had caught him in a few silly lies, boasting about who he was. Now God wanted Oscar to go and talk to him about being a pastor, which was something Oscar didn't even want to do.

This was too much for Oscar. Each day on his way to work, he would pass the church building and say, "No, I'm not going to do it." But God kept nudging him to talk to the pastor. One day, when he could stand it no longer, he made a deal with God, "Okay, Lord," he said," I will pull into the driveway, but if he is not in the parking lot, I will not knock on the door. I'm not going to spend any time looking for him."

He pulled into the parking lot, and just as he did, who walks out of the door? The pastor of course! Oscar tried to pull out without him noticing, but then he heard a voice calling "Hermano Oscar!" In his rear-view mirror, he could see the smiling man running after him. He sighed and reluctantly got out of the car and went to greet the pastor. He told him, "I don't know what you are going to think about this, but I have felt for many weeks that God has been calling me to pastor a church, and I was just now coming to see you about it." The pastor smiled and said, "Well, I'm not sure what it all means, but I will pray for you and let you know if God brings something to my attention." Oscar thanked him, got back in his car, upset with himself for even stopping, and drove home.

A few days later the pastor called our home and said, "Remember the conversation we had the other day? A pastor friend of mine in Centralia, Washington called and asked me if someone could come and cover for him while he and his family go on vacation for a few weeks." He went on to say that he found the whole thing a little odd. Why didn't the pastor just have one of the elders do it? But Oscar prayed and felt in his heart that this was what God wanted him to do, so he accepted the temporary job.

The church was in Centralia, Washington, which is about forty minutes north of where we were living in Castle Rock. The pastor wanted us to come a Sunday or two before he left, so that he could slowly hand the church over into our care. As time went by, we realized not everything was going well in that church. The pastor and the church did not see eye to eye and the pastor's real desire was to move permanently to the east coast where his wife's family lived.

We told the church that we would do a three-month trial to see if we were what they wanted. After three months, the vote was an overwhelming *yes*, and Oscar was officially made pastor of Iglesias Cristiana Resurección Church in Centralia, Washington. We weren't sure how this all fit in with the vision that God had given us for Honduras, but we pastored that church as faithfully as we knew how for four years. Through that time, we met and served some of the most wonderful people in the world, people who would later play a huge role in what God was doing in Honduras. Among them were many pastors and leaders who later made WWH2H the mission focus of their churches.

Over the next year, progress in Honduras moved slowly forward. In the United States getting your non-profit 501c3 certification is relatively easy. However, in Honduras it is much more challenging, and in order to be able to work legally in the country it is necessary to be a legal entity. We had applied, but the documentation was not moving forward. It was decided that our family would move to Honduras for six months to a year to establish H2H as a legal non-profit organization in the country. We had our assistant pastor take over in our absence. In September of 2001 we headed out with the Haas' to Honduras to start our journey of getting our ministry legalized in Honduras.

Over the next seven months, we worked diligently on securing the documents. I wish I could say we returned to Washington 'Mission accomplished', but it would be another four years before that would become a reality. While in Honduras, I injured my arm and needed to return to the United States for medical treatment.

In December 2002, Pastor Roy and Linda Henson resigned from the H2H board to focus on a new ministry they were developing based on a series of paintings that Linda had done after the 9/11 attacks. In January 2003, we gathered as a board and Mary was voted the new President of H2H and Dean and Rachel King joined the board of directors.

We met with a man from a nearby Longview church who specialized in helping churches and ministries get organized. He agreed to facilitate a workshop for our board to help us get focused in the right direction. In that meeting, we established our vision statement and made a five-year plan for the ministry. It was also in that meeting that the seed of the idea that our family should make a permanent move to Honduras was first planted.

By this time, we had been going to Honduras two to three times a year for the last five years. And while the project was advancing, it had never become anything more than a building project. When we would tell people we were building an orphanage in Honduras, they would say, "Oh, great, how is the one you built last year, doing?" No one realized it would take so long.

I can remember the day that Oscar told me, "Amy, I think it is time for us to go down fulltime." This was an interesting concept to me, because in all or our conversations about doing this ministry, I don't remember the idea of us going down to live there permanently ever coming up. Quite honestly, I figured someone with a degree or tons of experience would come along and be the one to go to Honduras to run this grand ministry. I have an 8th grade education; I had never even entertained that it would be us!

But isn't that just like God? If the person with the doctorate in psychology, with a minor in business administration, who speaks fluent English and Spanish, doesn't show up, well you've got to do it yourself! What we have learned over the years is that all along, God had planned to use His Holy Spirit in us to do this work. He would provide all the wisdom, funding, and help we needed.

In June of 2003 we loaded up our seven-passenger van, with a trailer in tow that Oscar had hand-built, and we headed to Honduras. Words can't describe how much I love road trips, and this was the road trip of a lifetime! We had our two daughters, Rachel and Sarah, and Oscar's mom with us. Rachel was three years old and Sarah was almost five. It took us exactly two weeks to drive from Washington State to Puerto Cortes, Honduras. We could have done it faster had we not gotten lost in Mexico, but that's another whole book! We arrived in Honduras on June 16th, 2003, and that was the beginning of the next phase of H2H.

Carey Anaya, Oscar, Lyle and Mary Frenter, Sarah, Amy, Rachel, and Rachel King

Oscar and Amy, and Pastor Tony and Claudia Anaya

7
Honduras Rising

"For my thoughts are not your thoughts, neither are your ways my ways, saith the Lord. For as the heavens are higher than the earth, so are my ways higher than your ways, and my thoughts than your thoughts." (Isaiah 55:8-9)

When we arrived in Honduras, we had nothing, but we were so excited! We lived with our good friends and ministry directors, Marcel and Elvia Almendarez, for the first few weeks. Eventually, we rented a small house in town and began the process of building this ministry.

One of our first objectives was getting the board of directors in Honduras established. We prayed that God would bring the people who He wanted to go forward in the ministry, and we invited people who Oscar knew in the area. Most had already been serving on the H2H board, which had been established when we submitted our paperwork for incorporation in Honduras a couple years earlier.

The first team we received as "Honduran residents" was the team of Lyle and Mary Frenter, who came to visit us in August 2003. That was one of the most pivotal points that this ministry has ever experienced. I don't think I fully realized what God was going to begin to teach us about ministry.

As typical Americans, we believed that before you can take kids in, you must have a fully built and furnished home, complete with water purification system, fire alarms, doctors and a psychologist on call, teachers, house staff and more. When we arrived in Honduras, the only construction that was completed on the five-pod building was the central pod on the bottom floor. It did not have windows or doors; it was just a concrete block frame. There was a separate building that we were putting up as well, that was going to serve as a medical clinic for the project.

One night, four days after the Frenters arrived in Honduras, Oscar took them into town to the internet café to use the phone and send and check email. When they arrived back at the house, all three had tears in their eyes. After we had pulled out of working with the first boys' orphanage in La Pita back in 1999, the project continued a few years, but eventually closed and the building became a retreat center for the church. I only know the fate of a few of the thirty boys who had lived in the home. One of the children we knew well from that project ended up back on the streets. His name was Edgar.

When we first met Edgar, he was an innocent little boy. I am not sure of his story, or why he lived at the orphanage, but that sweet little 9-year-old boy had now become a hardened 13-year-old, living on the streets and involving himself with the local gangs. We still believed, however, that there was hope for him. We repeatedly told him about the home we were building, and that he could come and live there just as soon as it was finished.

During that time, the Frenters introduced us to a friend of theirs who was a construction man with a huge heart, by the name of Steve Sharp. Each time Steve went down to Honduras, Oscar would take him into town to run errands and find the things they needed for the construction. On one of those trips in August of 2002, they ran into Edgar. Oscar introduced the two and explained Edgar's story to Steve.

Steve tells it this way, "He did not ask me for food. He did not ask me for money. He just wanted to know when his home would be ready." Steve took Edgar's picture, and then came home and told us of his encounter. He wrote to his friends saying that he was not going back to Honduras until he had raised the $50,000, we estimated we needed to finish the structure. Then he would go finish it and would not come back to the US until he had tucked Edgar into his bed in his new home. That photo of Edgar became our poster picture whenever we spoke at churches about the ministry over the next couple years.

One year later, as Oscar came through the door that night, he told me, "You should sit down. I have some bad news. Edgar is dead." My heart came up into my throat. "What happened?" I cried. Mary and Lyle simple sat on the couch with tears in their eyes and said, "We didn't act fast enough!"

I don't think any of us got much sleep that night. When Mary came into the kitchen the next morning her face was red, and her eyes were blood shot. She said, "I can't believe that we didn't get our act together fast enough to get him off the streets!" Edgar had crawled into the ventilation system of a local business to find a safe place to sleep. The business had been robbed a few times, and the owner had put up a very crude security system that basically consisted of live electrical wires at each possible entrance. Edgar was electrocuted, killed simply because he wanted to sleep and not be hurt by anyone. Is that any kind of a life for a little boy?

We spent the next several days crucifying ourselves for so many reasons, thinking: Perhaps we should not have pulled out of that orphanage. Perhaps we could have found a family who we could have paid to take Edgar into their home. But what about the 30 other boys who needed a home as well?

Hondurans are often hesitant to take in a young man who has been involved in gang activity. I remember talking about that very thing with Oscar when we first got to Honduras. We worried because we were moving down with our own two young daughters. But what did it matter now? He was dead, and there was no way to turn that around.

Mary Frenter shared the following thoughts with me about this time, as well as a poem she wrote in honor of Edgar.

Lyle and I had recently returned from Honduras. The second night we were there, we chanced to meet David on the streets of Puerto Cortes. We first met him in 2000, when he was living at the La Pita Orphanage. David, as well as three other former La Pita children, Wilson, Chicki, and Edgar, were scheduled to begin living at our unfinished Children's Home in Tegucigalpita the next week. Pastor Oscar Serrano, our Worldwide Heart to Heart Ministries Honduras National Director, was organizing a crew to learn building skills by working on our construction site. David told us Edgar had been killed the previous Saturday. We had not worked fast enough. Our hearts were broken.

We do not know much about Edgar's life from birth to age seven. Heart to Heart first meet him in 1999 when we sent a team to see how we could help after Hurricane Mitch. We found him living in the La Pita Orphanage run by the Holy Spirit Church of Honduras. H2H helped support that orphanage, and Edgar was there until 2001, when it closed due to fraudulent management. Thus, our current mission to build and manage our own home for those children.

From the age of nine, Edgar lived on the streets of Puerto Cortes, until his death at age eleven on August 3, 2003. He was electrocuted early Saturday morning by a live wire hanging in the vent of a supermarket, where he had sought shelter the night before. Edgar was born into a family, that, we guess, turned him out on the streets after Hurricane Mitch in 1998.

Many families were forced to do that at the time. Someone found him and placed him at the La Pita Orphanage. After it closed, he lived on the streets of Puerto Cortes, sleeping in doorways, surviving by whatever means he could. He had heard we were building a Children's Home. He knew he would have a place to live as soon as it was finished. He was just hanging on.

Last summer, he chanced to meet Steve Sharp, a H2H construction volunteer who was working on our Children's Home outside of Puerto Cortes. He noticed Steve's H2H shirt and, as Steve tells it, "He didn't ask me for money. He didn't ask me for food. He just wanted to know, 'When will my home be ready?'"

"O the depth of the riches both of the wisdom and knowledge of God! How unsearchable are his judgments, and his ways past finding out!" (Romans 11:33)

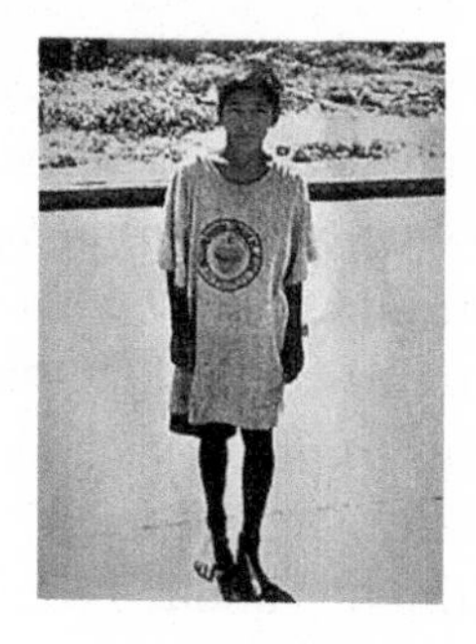

Edgar is Finally Home

In Memory of Edgar Who Posed the Question, "When Will My Home Be Ready?"
Born 1992 - Died August 3, 2003.

You had no safe place to lay your head,
No one to hold you when you were afraid,
No one to fix your favorite meal,
"When will my home be ready?"
Finding your comforts all by yourself,
No time to play and have fun,
No parents, no love, no one to care,
"When will my home be ready?"
Spurred on by that question, we desperately sought
The way to prepare that home.
But God had a different plan for this child,
And took Edgar home with Him.
He no longer has to beg on the streets,
To feel fear and be all alone,
We know with assurance he rests in the arms,
Of His loving Father in Heaven.
The Home we are building was not meant to be,
For this child who posed the question.
But there are so many more little Edgars just waiting
And hoping we won't be too late.
Please Lord, touch the hearts of your children of plenty,
Who have the means and the way,
To help us finish "Edgar's Home" in the country,
So that by all means, some might be saved.

Mary Frenter

We tried to find where they had taken his body, but because we were not family, the body was sent to San Pedro Sula to be used for science. We didn't really understand what we had done wrong. We had worked as hard as we could and didn't know what we could have done differently. The Frenters returned to the United States with the promise that we would get this thing done.

It was just a few days after they left, when Mary called us and said that she was showering and thinking about those children wandering around the dangerous streets, desperately searching for their basic needs. The God inspired thought came to her, "We should at least begin to feed them." Wrapped in a towel, she went into her kitchen where Lyle was making the morning coffee. He looked up and said to her, "Honey, we at least need to begin feeding these kids."

It was a God confirmation! Oscar and I had been thinking the same thing. The whole tragic event of losing Edgar served to wake us up. There was no reason for Edgar to die! We had a building in Tegucigalpita. Perhaps, it was just a block frame with no doors, windows, beds, nothing. However, it was a place to sleep in safety. We decided that if there were kids out there, and they needed a safe place to sleep, there was no reason for another child to die.

Oscar had a good friend who was out of work at the time, and he agreed to go out to the Tegucigalpita project, with air mattresses, and live with and be a house father to any boys who needed to be there. Immediately, we found two young boys who were good friends of Edgar's, who also lived on the streets. In those days we didn't know what we were doing; however, we weren't going to let that stop us.

We did not tell the boys that they would be coming to an "orphanage", because we knew what the word "orphanage" meant to most of them. We simply said that we had a building project going on way out in Tegucigalpita. We were building an orphanage, and we would give them a job to help us. We told them that they would have to live out there, because it was a two-hour drive before the new road was built. Our first two boys were Eduardo and Manuel, who were both twelve years old. They came to live at the project. We got air mattresses, and Mary contacted some family members who provided money to buy food and other things that we needed.

The boys told us about another boy who had come to live under the bridge just recently, and they thought he might like to come as well. They went to find him. His name was Josué, and he was thirteen years old. We thought the easiest thing to do was to let the boys live on the bottom floor of the center building and work on getting the clinic building finished, so that could eventually be their house. One thing that Lyle had always said was, "Once you get kids, people will begin to support this ministry." His prophecy turned out to be very true. Support started to come in; groups came down and the construction of the project moved forward.

Finally, the clinic was finished and converted into a three-bedroom house. Manuel told us about his little brother Norman who was nine years old and living in a garbage dumpster by the market. We found him, and he began his life with us as well. I remember that first Christmas, when we bought the boys bunk beds and pillows. I will never forget a conversation that I overheard between Norman and his brother Manuel about how wonderful it was to sleep in a bed with a pillow!

It was at that same time that we realized just how many children lived on the streets of Puerto Cortes. They were all over, however, not all of them were "homeless". Many of them were the children from the dump. The local garbage dump was also home to about 100 families. Most shared the same story; single prostitute mother, stair-step kids, homes made of tin, sticks and other items found in the garbage. The kids would flood into the city during the day and beg at street corners and restaurants. We could see that these children faced the same dangerous, life-threatening situations that Edgar had faced, while simply looking for their basic needs to be met.

At that time, we decided that we did not have the resources to take them all in, but we could feed them. Mary once again went to anyone and everyone she knew and collected the funds to start the "Meals from the Heart" program. Elvia Almendarez and I would cook a lunch each day for about eighty to one hundred children from the slums and dump areas. A friend allowed us to use a picnic area that he owned, free of charge, with serving tables and restaurant style tables and chairs. We would cook the meal at Elvia's house, and then drive out to serve it. Each day we would arrive to find at least fifty to eighty hungry little children. It was a hard but wonderful time for me. Back in those days, my Spanish was practically non-existent. But each day, working with Elvia and her three children, I learned how to speak. Also, thanks to Elvia's amazing cooking skills, I learned the wonder of incredible Honduran cuisine.

I used the time to teach the kids as many things as I could think of. Each day, they would learn a new word in English. We would pray with them, teach them about Jesus, and sit with and counsel them. The feeding program ran for one year and was an amazing time of learning for all of us.

You never know what your simple" little mustard seed" can do. After the feeding program ended, the dump was walled off and the mayor relocated the residents of the dump to another area at the back of town. I didn't see the kids at all after the program ended. One day, about two years later, I was in town running some errands, when I heard a woman's voice calling me from behind. "Hermana Amy!" she called. I saw a woman with a teenage girl running toward me. When they reached me, they both embraced me with kisses. I, of course, was feeling very embarrassed, because I didn't really remember who they were. "Don't you remember us from the feeding program?" the woman asked. "And look, this is Cristiana." Oh yes, Cristiana, now I remembered!

Standing before me was a beautiful sixteen-year-old young woman who didn't even resemble the young girl I had met three years earlier. Cristiana would come to the feeding program each day for lunch. She was a pretty little girl, but it was hidden behind the very sour expression she always wore. She was one of the angriest young ladies I had ever met. One day she came to the feeding program with a huge black eye. I begged her, as did Oscar, to tell us what was going on and who did this to her. She just kept saying that she fell, but you knew she was covering something up. She wasn't angry, but scared, as we pressed her for the truth about her injuries. I simply told her, "I understand you don't want to - or can't - talk about it, just let me pray for you." So, we prayed together, as tears rolled down her cheeks. And now, here she was standing before me with something I had never seen before, a big beautiful smile! But not just any smile, it was one of those smiles that you know comes from the inside.

We spent several moments getting caught up. Cristiana was now in her last year of high school and dreaming of going to college. As we said our goodbyes, Cristiana embraced me one last time and said, "I thank you so much for everything. I pray for you every day." Wow! It is those kinds of encounters that keep you going when the going gets tough!

First boys living at the children's village in Tegucigalpita

Boy's house under construction

The boys living at the village and others who helped with the construction

Food Program: Giving free food to children who are in need

8

I Ran All Night!

"But verily God hath heard me; he hath attended to the voice of my prayer." (Psalm 66:19)

One day a friend of Oscar's asked if he could take a man who had a ministry filming other ministries to visit and film the Village. Oscar thought that would be fine and drove out to the border to pick them up. They arrived late at night, and it was raining. We took them for some dinner at Pizza Hut in Puerto Cortes and talked about our ministry and our plans.

I remember the night so well. It was in November, the peak of the Honduran rainy season, and it was coming down in buckets. Around 11 pm, just as we were leaving, a young boy appeared out of nowhere asking for money. Oscar talked to the young man, who told us that his name was Marlon. He said he lived behind the restaurant beside the garbage dumpster.

Oscar told him we had a building project going on out in Tegucigalpita and that he could come help us there. They arranged for Oscar to come and pick up him the next day at 8 am. We gave him the left-over pizza, and said we would come, bright and early the next morning, to pick him up. We weren't surprised when he didn't show up. But don't worry, it wasn't the last that we would see of him.

I often thought of him and worried about him. One day, as we were serving food at the feeding program, a new young man showed up to eat. He was dirty and very sick. He had an ear infection that was so bad you could see if from the outside. At that time, I did not recognize him, but Oscar recognized him immediately. We asked him why he didn't show up that day, and as we expected, he told us he was afraid. He only came for food that day because he had no other options.

He was now ready to take a chance on us, change his life, and go to the Village. That day, he climbed into our car and went out to Tegucigalpita. Marlon was only nine years old at that time. He grew up with us at the Village and became a wonderful young man, graduated high school and hopes to one day be an electrician. Marlon met Sarah who came to Honduras from Oregon as a young teenager on mission trips. She returned to Honduras to work at our school in 2011. In 2012, Marlon and Sarah were married. They now live in Oregon but hope to return to Honduras to continue to serve.

The project continued to grow. More teams came down to Honduras and more financial sponsors for the kids were found. One day a young man showed up at the Village and told us that his name was Marvin. He was from a village up in the mountains called Las Flores and was looking for a place to start his life over. One of the men who had helped us with much of the building was a mason named Miguel. He was from the same mountain village as Marvin. Miguel had come down from the mountains of Honduras to the village of Tegucigalpita when a friend found him a job. Miguel was unmarried and not a Christian when he started to work for us in the construction of the Children's Village.

Miguel was an amazingly hard worker. Oscar never preached to him on the job; he simply shined the light before him. Miguel watched and worked next to many "gringos" in those days and began to wonder, "What are they doing here?" He told us later, that he was so confused. Why would these people, living comfortably in the United States, want to come here and do this?

One day, he pulled Oscar aside and asked, "What is this really all about? What's the angle? What's the catch? What are they really trying to get out of this?" In Miguel's life there was only one motto, "Save yourself!" Oscar told him, "Well, we are doing this, because Jesus did it for us." Miguel decided then and there, he wanted this Jesus for himself and asked the Lord into his heart. Miguel later married, and he and his wife have three children. They serve on the leadership of their church. Miguel still serves as construction foreman on all our building projects.

Now Miguel had Marvin standing in front of him, asking for help. However, he had none to give. He told Marvin that he should talk to the directors of this ministry, because they worked with children, and maybe they could give him something. Marvin found Oscar and asked Oscar for the opportunity to be a part of the Village. Oscar's initial response was no, because he was already almost fifteen years old, too old, we thought, to be a part of our program.

Marvin had grown up in an extremely poor part of the world, as Honduras is the second poorest country in the Western Hemisphere, but Marvin was poor even by Honduran standards. He grew up angry and without hope. This hopelessness caused him to look for anything that would be a way out of poverty. He became the enemy of the state in his home village. Marvin often stole from his neighbors and caused problems for his family.

Things went from bad to worse in Marvin's life. He joined gangs and went around Honduras committing crimes and carrying weapons. Marvin had become a full-time gang member and used drugs and alcohol. Though it had taken him out of his extreme poverty, Marvin always knew that was not who he really was. Then one day, he decided he had to change. He went to look for Miguel.

Marvin was not going to take no for an answer and persisted each day. Oscar finally told him, go back to your home and get a letter from your parents giving us permission to have you here and be back by tomorrow. Oscar was certain that this would throw him off, as he didn't think he could even make it there and back in one day. But to Oscar's surprise, when he showed up at the project the next day, there was Marvin waiting for him with letter in hand. I later asked Marvin how he made it back so soon. He told me, "I ran all night!" Marvin was added to our growing family.

Marvin truly "grew up" at the Village and became, not just a son, but a great friend. He met a young woman, Karen, from the United States who began coming to Honduras on mission trips as a teenager. She and Marvin married in 2010, and now live in her hometown in Tennessee. When she and Marvin returned to Honduras, he came prepared with funds and repaid each person he had stolen from in his home village. They also began a small ministry repairing homes in Las Flores. The couple had their first son, Tomas, on Marvin's birthday, May 15th, 2014, and two years later were blessed with a daughter. Marvin had been changed by a great God!

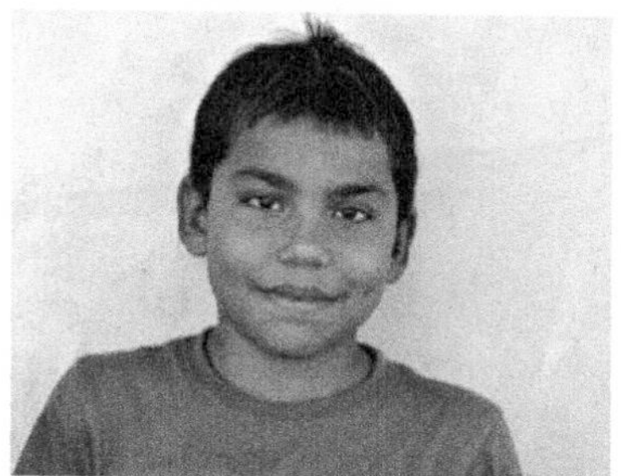

Marlon Manzanares - 2003

Sarah & Marlon's wedding
Portland, OR 2015

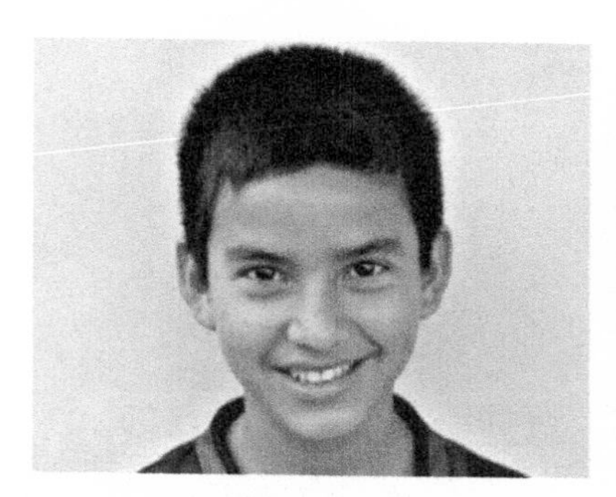

Marvin- 2003

Marvin Ramos Family

Marvin and Karen's wedding
Tennessee 2010

9

God's Plan Is Bigger Than Our Plan

"For my thoughts are not your thoughts, neither are your ways my ways, saith the Lord." (Isaiah 55:8)

Back in those early days, we didn't have phones. Honduras has come long way in just a short time. There were not even cell phones back then. To make phone calls or send emails, we had to go to the telephone company, and then internet cafés began to pop up.

One night we went into a local internet café to make some phone calls. Oscar noticed all the young children using the computers to watch pornography, and no one seemed to care. Oscar was irate and told the young man working at the desk that he was going to report this to the authorities. However, the owners of the café found us and apologized for what was happening. They explained that they did not know what was going on when they weren't in the café and thanked us for bringing it to their attention. The next time we went in, we noticed signs throughout the café stating that it was prohibited for anyone under the age of eighteen to enter those sites.

The café owner's family contacted us again, this time to ask for help with their nephews. The owner, Rosalinda, told us that her brother had three young sons he was raising alone. He was a shell of a man, a chronic alcoholic. The aunt took us to see the place where they lived, and I can't even begin to describe it. The aunt could not take them into her house, because she already had fourteen people living in their very humble two-bedroom home. Her husband said no more could come.

We had a big problem. When we had outlined the plan for the Village, we had decided we were going to be a boys' home and could not take "handicapped" children, because we did not have the resources to care for them properly. Out of these three boys, two were handicapped. David, age four, had a club foot and his brother, Cesar was mentally challenged. But we had learned two important things from our experience with Edgar: first, there was not some other more well-established place that was already built for children with such challenges. We were it. And second, these children did not have time on their side. So, we took the boys in and prayed for God to give us the wisdom and grace to give them what they needed.

The next children that God brought us challenged our second decision to take in only boys. These new children were Adonis, Nelson and their older sister, Ilcy. We decided that we would take the boys, but that we would look for another home for Ilcy. There was a girls' home in Omoa, a town twenty miles east of our Village, but we learned that Honduras law does not allow you to separate siblings, a policy that we highly respect. The children had been living on the streets with their alcoholic father. The boys were both under five years old, and Ilcy was only seven. All three of the kids were at risk from predators in the streets, sickness, and the outside elements. They were also suffering from malnutrition. So, as God would have it, we were now officially a boys' home, a girls' home, and a home for the handicapped.

Little did we know that the ministry was about to take a quantum leap. A pastor friend, by the name of Ed Miller, from our old hometown of Castle Rock, Washington, had come down on several occasions for crusades and medical teams. He had a friend who he had mentored as a young man. He was a businessman from Washington State who owned several gas stations along the I-5 corridor and an oil company. Pastor Ed, who was also a construction man, was doing a job for this gentleman. When it was done, the businessman asked, "How much do I owe you?" Pastor Ed said, "A trip to Honduras". He told him that payment for him would be that he travel with him to Honduras to see the project. He was more than happy to do so.

Pastor Ed later told us that when this man was a young Christian, just out of college, he had two choices. His real heart was to become a missionary, but his father wanted him to take over the oil business that he had started. He asked Pastor Ed for council, and he told him, "Perhaps if you are financially well-off you can be a help to missions." So, the man decided to take his father's business. Ed was now showing him how he could also be a missionary.

The man, along with his two children and Pastor Ed came in December 2003 for a very quick four-day trip to Honduras. During that time, they worked at the feeding program, visited the Village and saw the dump and slum areas. At this point, we had calculated that it would cost us about $50,000 to finish the building.

One day, while Pastor Ed and his friend were in town, we decided to stop at a local restaurant that was on the beach. They could swim in the Caribbean and get some good Honduran food. As we were dining, a man I had never met before, came up and introduced himself as the land team mission coordinator from Mercy Ships International. He said that he heard us talking and knew that we were Christians and wanted to introduce himself.

We told him who we were, and he said he had been out to the Tegucigalpita campus years ago, as he was driving through. He had seen it several times and had understood through some locals that it was a Christian project and would be an orphanage. He told us that one of his teams had stopped at the property, got out of their cars and prayed for the project. What his department of Mercy Ships did was to go into countries and help with existing projects such as ours. He told us that he thought he could get some teams together and help us with the future construction. Pastor Ed's friend asked him, "How much money do you have in mind for this?" He responded, "Oh, probably somewhere around $25,000." At that point, Pastor Ed's friend said, "Okay, I'll match that." God had just provided the $50,000!

Oscar and I could not believe what we were hearing! The

building was going to get finished, and we had the pledges and promises to get it done. The team returned home, and we called Mary right away and celebrated together. Both sides were good for their word. Within a few months, Mercy Ships sent their first team. By this time the former director had moved on from the ministry, and it was now being overseen by Gary and Sylvia Thacker.

The Thacker's were amazing people! Gary had tattoos from head to toe and one of the most amazing testimonies I have ever heard. He was an ex-biker in the vintage car restoration business, when God called him and his wife, a certified nurse, to the missions' business. Mercy Ships was not able to give the $25,000 right away, but they gave something much better, seven years of assistance including sending at least fifty teams, thousands of dollars in projects at the Village, and more than anything else, a very dear friendship and partnership with this ministry that continues today.

Ed's friend delivered and how! Over the next twelve months, he and his oil business friends and contacts blessed the ministry with over $60,000, and the home was built. In addition, this man had several good friends in the medical field. Within months, the first of their medical teams was on their way to Honduras, and many still come each year.

Each day the project changed and grew. New people and churches were getting involved. By this time, we had boys and girls, and those boys and girls were growing up. If there is anything that I regret, it's not having been able to study psychology. The children now started coming from the government and government orphanages. Many of them were taken out of their homes because of severe abuse. Many of them had suffered physical, verbal and sexual abuse. A few of them could say that their first sexual partner was a member of their own family. They were incredibly needy.

I learned then and there that there were many things in life that were much bigger than Amy Serrano of Plaquemine, Louisiana.! You can only imagine the kinds of problems that arise when you have teenage boys and teenage girls, all with emotional problems, living together. We were sure this was not going to work, and they themselves would create new residents. The young men even asked

Oscar to get the girls out of there! They told him they were trying to be good boys, but the girls were all over them!

We began to pray about a way of separating them. We were hoping to find an entirely separate piece of property, but we had no money. We set a deadline and prayed that God would show us what we were to do. We said that if we did not have the property by a certain date, we would build the girls' home at the back end of the village property. We had eight acres of land and were currently only using about 1 acre at the front end. We figured that we could put a fence between the two ends and build the girls home as far away from the boys as possible.

That is what we did. The building would take some time to build. Since the need to get the boys and girls separated was urgent, we decided to find a home near us in town to rent, so the girls could move into it. The house that we rented was owned by a friend of ours, and it was in the same neighborhood as the house that we lived in. It was nice to have the girls close by. They came over to my house each day. We gave them money to do small jobs around the house. Maria, the house mother in charge, told me that each of the girls asked her to hold their money. Although it was only about $5 a month, each girl gave all their pay to their birth mothers and siblings to help with their needs back in the villages they had come from.

We began to learn about the extremely intricate and complicated psyche of children. In many cases, it didn't matter how much abuse their parents had subjected them to, they still held extreme loyalty to them. Many of the kids were their own worst enemy. Their biggest challenge was not lack of food or shelter; it was fighting their own demons. I guess we had a fantasy that we would come down to Honduras and build this beautiful home where these kids would be so happy and so thankful. We really knew nothing! The fact is it was far from the fantasy we had imagined it would be. One of the hardest things for the kids to accept was structure. This was clearly brought to our attention by a young woman named Iris who came to the Village.

When Iris initially came, INHFA, the Honduran equivalent of

Child Protective Services in the United States, told us that she was probably pregnant by her father. Iris sat with Oscar and me and told us the horror stories of the abuse, when it started, and how it all happened. However, Iris, only fourteen years old, also let us know from the beginning that she did not want to go to school. She wanted us to employ her to help take care of the younger girls. We told her that we were sorry, but that was not how things worked at the Village. She would have to go to school and live with the schedule of all the other kids.

One day we received a phone call from Maria, one of our ministry workers, telling us that Iris had run away that night. We reported this to the authorities, and they called us back later to tell us that she had been found. Guess where? She was at her Dad's house. She had gone back home. Why? Because at our place, she had to wake up at 5:30 am, get showered, eat breakfast, do chores, go to school, come home, go to bed at a certain hour, and so on. She had to live with a schedule and with responsibilities. In her dad's house, she could sleep in all day, go out with no responsibilities, and stay out at the pool hall with her boyfriends all night. She just had to be willing to take the abuse. And when it all came down to it, the abuse was familiar, she knew what to expect and what to do with it. But the structure was unknown and stifling, and she just could not accept it.

I usually knew right away the difference between a kid who was going to "make it" and one that would not, simply by seeing where their hearts were. When a ten-year-old child came in talking about how the bus station in San Pedro Sula was the "domain" for him and his gang, and went on to glorify street life, we knew that it would take a miracle, and there have been many, for him to make it through. But it has been these kids that have taught us grace and the glory of God. It's human nature to try and be the savior.

Many kids have come into our home, and we have invested years into their lives, only to wake up one morning to find they took off. God has told us time and time again that we are not the saviors, we are simply the tools that He uses. These children are on a journey that is God designed, and He will rise as the Savior! We are just a part of their journey, not the whole thing. We do our best to give them all that we can, and in the end, that gift is not given in vain. They picked up something, something that will take them forward on that journey.

We are hard heads and the Lord knows that, so sometimes He brings us to the places He wants us to go to teach us that only He is really in charge. Our only job is to blindly follow Him, believing in faith.

Boys from the children's village

Gary and Silvia Thacker

Nelson, Ilcy, and Adonis

10

Will Train the Right Person

"Which in time past were not a people, but are now the people of God: which had not obtained mercy, but now have obtained mercy." (1 Peter 2:10)

We were now into the year 2006. Three years of ministry and what the Lord had done so far was beyond our imagination. Twenty-five children were now out of harm's way, receiving good food and feeling the results of their answered prayers. The most interesting thing that the Lord was doing in all of this was, He was taking nothing and turning it into something. You know how you see those certain types of people that are what I like to call "kid magnets"? You know what I mean, the people who sit down in a crowd, and suddenly, they are drowning in children. I am *not* one of those people. I have always seen children as the most vulnerable members of our society. I have always felt deeply burdened to defend their rights, but I never thought that I had great talent in dealing with kids directly.

It was in these early years that I learned to appreciate the old saying that became famous in the classified ad section, "will train the right person". The reality is that none of us running H2H, either in the United States or in Honduras had the education or skills that one would need to do what we did. It only makes it that much more of a finger pointing in the direction of God. It was, is, and always will be HIM who is the Savior of these kids; we are all just privileged participants in His plan. The moment we became the right people, empty of self and completely reliant on God, and more than anything out of HIS way, HE trained us and was faithful to give us all that we needed. We were thrown into the "University of Child Care", where the children were our professors. The good news is, they were excellent teachers!

Going into 2006, we were getting to know the "business", what worked and what didn't. We came to recognize the unique psyche of children. Taking children off the streets was easy; it could be done in one day, however, taking the street out of the child takes years. It is difficult to fully explain what the profound need of the Honduran child is in one book. Honduras, at the time I am writing this book, is the second poorest nation in the western hemisphere after Haiti. In addition, at the same time, Honduras holds an unfortunate title: it is the most violent country in the world! In 2013, more civilians died due to violent crime per capita in San Pedro Sula, Honduras, than in Iraq in 2007 at the height of the insurgency.

The reasons for this are profound. They cover the whole gamut of economics and politics, but mostly it is spiritual. When you spend any real time in Honduras and can see just below the lush tropical façade, you will see a place where hope is long gone. Generations of desperation have given birth to a spirit of hopelessness, which brings a nation into survival mode. Many of these kids are in a damned situation, and there is nothing they can do to get out of it.

Education is not an option, and hard work will only wear out their youth. Young men have the option of working days of extremely hard labor in the fields with a machete and will still not make enough money to put a little bit of beans and rice on the table. For many parents, the best that they can give their kids is to bring them out to work beside them in the fields, with no hope of going to school. But those kids are the lucky ones. Many other kids don't even have that. They are forced to go out to the streets, pushed out by their parents who can no longer care for them.

These young people have a sad choice. They can kill themselves in hard labor with no hope, or they can take option number two. This option includes having a car, the best cell phone, and nice clothes, and means becoming a gang member. For many children growing up in gang infested communities or on the streets, joining the gangs is not even a personal choice; they are forced into membership. In these poor communities, young boys are targeted to become soldiers for the organization.

Young girls, on the other hand, are forced into prostitution and trafficking rings at a young age. The children's homes and orphanages are all over-crowded and quite honestly, more harm can be done to a child in one of these public orphanages, than they often face on the streets. I have heard of children that survived somewhat well on the streets yet were violently raped or beaten in the orphanages. We have dealt with children less than ten years old who had already murdered for their gangs. And we have dealt with young girls, pregnant by their fathers. I am sorry to say, I think we have seen it all.

With no protection from the authorities, who unfortunately sometimes play for the wrong team, they have no one to defend or protect them. One in four children suffers from some form of malnutrition. Historically, the biggest killer of children in Honduras has been diarrhea, caused by parasitic infestations that are completely treatable.

That said; let me tell you the most amazing thing. Where sin is, grace does much more abound! We read the Bible and hear the magnificent stories of the blind seeing, the deaf hearing, the lame walking, and the dead coming back to life. I am here to testify; we have seen it! It defies all laws of logic and science that anyone could ever really come back from these types of horrific atrocities. Yet, not only do we see these kids coming back, we see them thriving!

While working in Honduras, we have had one goal, to see His kingdom come and His will be done in Honduras as it is in Heaven. We have seen incredible miracles. We have seen blind receiving sight, new organs growing, incurable illnesses healing and the rain stopping at a command. However, there is not a miracle more amazing to me than watching God bring the dead spirit back to life in one of our children. They may have had a curse spoken over them and had a destiny of destruction, and to that I only have one thing to say: But God!

God has always been faithful and true. The project grew each day. Throughout those years, we were busy building what is now the boys' home on the Tegucigalpita campus. More churches joined in, more people joined in, and more kids came to be part of the family. We prayed for someone who could care for our kids' medical needs, and along came Kim Sharp. Her husband Steve had been instrumental in the building of the boys' house. She came and has continued to come, almost every year since, to keep our kids' health charts up to date.

We prayed for someone to take care of their teeth. Many of these kids came to us badly in need of dental care. One child had over thirty-two cavities. There was no way that we could afford to get them the care they needed. Imagine, twenty-five children averaging ten cavities each! But God! He sent us Medical Relief International for that time, a ministry from Seattle, Washington and Antioch Bible Church. They came with dentists, hygienists, oral surgeons and all the equipment needed and pulled, filled, cleaned and polished, not just for our kids, but also for our workers.

We also continued our outreach to the local community in the form of medical teams and Vacation Bible School (VBS) teams. Our VBS teams were often headed by Tina Campbell and Carol Rutledge, two amazing missionaries who always impressed me with their faith. Our VBS. teams would set up in local schools and put an invitation out to entire communities. One year, in just one day, our VBS. was attended by nearly 600 children, with only about twenty adult staff! It was chaotic, but beautiful. We always did our best to love and cherish the kids. Over the years, we have witnessed thousands of children invite the Lord into their hearts.

The medical teams were much the same; we would go into very remote mountain villages to give much needed medical care. We would often take doctors, nurses, dentists, and optometrists to care for some of the poorest people in the world. Many had never seen a doctor or a dentist in their whole lives. Often, there was not much we could do for them. Funguses, rashes, skin wounds, parasites, scabies, aches and pains, and rotten teeth, were the usual maladies.

Things such as high blood pressure, diabetes and more profound illnesses, were out of our hands.

However, I noticed what the people really wanted was to simply know that we cared. They felt that the medicines brought by "gringo" doctors were superior to Honduran drugs. People would walk hours to get to the medical brigades. You could tell that the families, though extremely poor, dressed their children in their absolute best clothes. Even if they were stained and torn, they always came clean. You could tell that this visit was especially important to them. And if it was important to them, I made sure it was important to me! The medical teams were also the vehicle we used to bring the gospel. Each patient was prayed for and received the plan of salvation. Hundreds have received the Lord over the years.

That year we also started a small clinic at the Village. A friend of Oscar's from childhood had become a nurse and agreed to work at the Village each day attending to the daily needs of the kids. The medications and a small salary for the nurse, were covered by paying patients from the community. We also finally got our Articles of Incorporation in Honduras that year. We had applied for it in the year 2000 and six years later, we finally made our way through the red tape of the government bureaucracy. It was crucially important to have these papers, because without them, we legally could do nothing. We received our first container that year from the United States. That was interesting! I don't think I have ever seen so many headless baby dolls, toy cars with no wheels on them, or unusable clothing. We have really learned a lot!

We were about to learn that all of this comes with its own dangers. Another ministry we had served with on medical missions, contacted us about a family that their medical team had just served. It was a family of three children who lived with their grandmother, who they believed was suffering from mental illness, and their father, who was reportedly dangerous and violent.

The team visited the home of the children and were shocked at the conditions they were living in. The biggest concern was for the youngest of the clan. He was eight years old and only weighed thirty-eight pounds. He had a condition called prolapsed bowel syndrome.

It is life threatening if not treated. In this condition, a child literally "poops" out their guts. When the child would have a bowel movement, much of his intestines would come out with it. We had to put on a glove and put everything back in. And his bowel movements were basically filled with blood and worms. All of this is caused by pica, a condition that drives a person to eat dirt, and that results in them contracting parasitic illnesses.

Oscar and I decided to go to their home to see the situation for ourselves. When we arrived, Oscar asked me to wait in the car while he checked it out. We had to park a long distance from the home, because you had to walk up a narrow, steep path on the mountain side for a considerable distance in order to reach it. Once there, Oscar found the grandmother and the three children. He told her that the kids could come to live at the Village and be well cared for and the youngest would get the health care he needed to survive. It was plain to see that the grandmother suffered troubled thinking, but she agreed that the kids should come to live at the Village with us. We needed to get the documents together to legally have the kids live at the Village and told the grandmother we would be back soon.

Just as Oscar was about to leave, the children's father arrived. The rumor that we heard from locals was that, in the past, the father had killed people. He was angry and irrational. When he arrived back at his home, he had a machete in his hand. Oscar carefully explained that he was in their home to find out if the children could go to a safer place to improve their health. The father, with machete in hand, told Oscar that someone was going to die that day. He told him that those were his children and lifted his hand threateningly at Oscar. Oscar told us later that the children were crouched down in the corner shaking with fear.

Oscar abruptly excused himself from their home and made his panicked way back to the car. He said it is only by the grace of God that he got out and doesn't know how or why the man did not follow him. We now knew that those kids were in real danger, and we had to do something soon. We made our way to the police station and reported all that had happened. The next day, we returned to the home, this time with the police at our sides. When we arrived, the father was not home, so the grandmother and the children packed their few things and headed out with the police officers.

The youngest child continued to be extremely ill. We took him to the hospital almost every day. His condition was serious, and, we did not know how long he would last. The doctors told us the same thing each day; there was not much that could be done for him. Only time would heal his intestinal wounds. The truth is time never healed his wounds. To this day he suffers with digestive problems and there are many foods he cannot eat. At seventeen, he is only ninety pounds and stands only 4'9". But today he is a wise, wonderful, alive young man with THE most beautiful smile I have ever seen! The doctors say that had he not received the medical care that he did, when he did, he would not have lasted another month.

Just months after we removed the children from the home, a group of men who the father owed money to, entered their home and killed both him and his mother. We are sure that, had the children been there, they would have been killed, as well.

As awareness of the ministry grew in the United States, it also grew in Honduras and other Hondurans and other nationalities came to help us. The beach resort where our teams stayed was owned by two wonderful Christian people from Columbia. From the beginning, they were concerned for our kids and very compassionate regarding what we were doing. They began that year to donate vegetables to the ministry. It started as just vegetables, but grew to be chicken, cereals, fruits and grains. We also became more organized with our board of directors in Honduras. Marcel Almendarez and his wife Elvia have been with us from the beginning and still serve by our side to this day, along with Rafael Valle, who was part of our work force in Honduras until his death in 2014.

In the mist of all this, we had yet another piece that the Lord was putting into place. Before we went to Honduras, we had pastored the church in Washington State, but now that we were in Honduras, it was nice to simply arrive at church and be fed. We started attending an Assemblies of God Church in town and were incredibly happy spiritually. Our board members, however, were not. They were all members of the church that my husband grew up in.

In 1999 the pastor of that church, who was a good friend of Oscars, was killed in an accident at his work. After Pastor Juan's death, the church hired new pastors, but none seemed to fit. Finally, in 2004, the church decided to disband, and all the members moved on to different churches. Most however, said that it was never the same. They had been a church family for many years, and now they all felt that they were without a spiritual home. They would often sit with Oscar and ask questions about the Bible and Christian living. They eventually asked if he would lead a Bible study for them. At first Oscar said no, because we were already so busy with the ministry. Finally, they wore Oscar out and he agreed.

The church that we were attending met in the evenings, so we could meet with them on Sunday morning. That first morning, in October 2006, I put on my ten-cup coffee pot, and set eight chairs around my kitchen table. Forty people showed up! The next week it was closer to sixty people and the week after that it was much the same. On the third or fourth week, there was an elderly woman in the group who was ill, so we asked one of the men if he would lead a prayer for her. He stood to his feet and began to pray saying, "Lord thank you so much for our sister that is ill, we ask you to heal her, and we thank you for our new church!" At first, I was wondering where his new church might be, before I realized that he was talking about us! We had been had! We reluctantly agreed to this and said that we would do it for a few months, but that would be it. Today, eight years later, the church is 250 members strong and has become the extended family for all our kids.

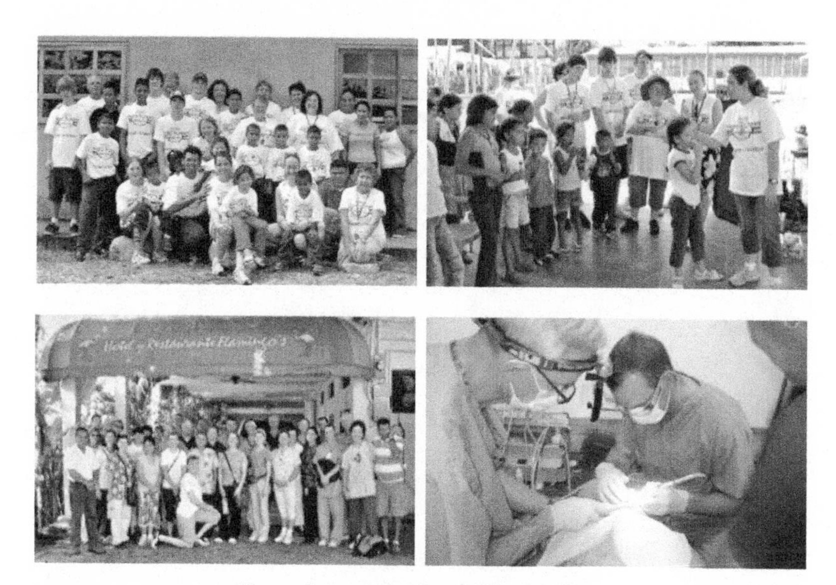

Teams that served at the Children's Village

Marcos, Daniela, and Jehovanny

11

But God!

"And he said unto me, My grace is sufficient for thee: for my strength is made perfect in weakness.'" (2 Corinthians 12:9a)

In July of 2007, we were looking at our child David, who I mentioned previously in this book. He had come to us in 2005 with his brothers, Cesar who was mentally handicapped, and his other older brother, Mauricio. David had a club foot condition that could have been easily fixed when he was born. His mother was a prostitute, who abandoned him when he was a baby, and his father died from alcoholism. The aunt brought us to the home where they lived. It was unbelievable. The home was a tiny shack which was a one room building built over a swamp. The aunt told us the children would often go out and play and come back covered in leeches.

Upon entering the home, all you saw was a single mattress that was totally black and soiled. The boys slept there every night, and due to their respective issues, wet the bed nightly. Doctors told the aunt that David could walk for now, because he was small. But if he did not have corrective surgery, he would end up in a wheelchair. When the boys came to live with us, we immediately went to work trying to find the surgery this child needed.

Through several connections, we finally found him the care he needed at the Shriner's Hospital in Portland, Oregon. Only months before we were hoping to send David to the states, a team from Washington State came to donate backpacks to kids in need. One of the team members was Denise Bardal; she loved David from the moment she met him. Denise agreed to host David in their home during the time that he would have his surgeries, and soon David was on his way to Portland.

All was going well for him and his surgeries. His condition was going to require many surgeries and therapy. During that time, his long-lost mother, who had run away to be a prostitute in Guatemala when David was a baby, unexpectedly showed up again. She was clearly unstable, but she had gone to the authorities and said that they were her kids and she wanted them back. The mother had found work, cleaning houses for a friend of the police chief. This friend encouraged the police chief to pull the kids out of the home and bring them back to the mom. They showed up with armed guards at the Village and told us we needed to hand over the three children. Next, they drove over to the kids' school, dragging them out of the classroom as the kids cried, begging to stay. The teacher was also following them out of the class, crying and begging the authorities not to take the children.

To this day, the oldest brother is a twenty-three-year-old crazy man who lives on the streets of Puerto Cortes, and the middle brother is a hardened gang member who has been deeply involved in crime. We knew that if we brought David back to Honduras from the United States, his mother would take him back as well. She was using the boys to beg in the streets to maintain herself, and David would be forced to do the same. We kept David in the States until things with his mother changed.

In 2009, the mother came to us and asked us about the possibility of us taking the middle child back. By this time, however, it had become impossible. The young man was already in trouble with the law, and we knew that we could not bring him to the Children's Village and mix him in with the small children we had living there. We knew it was time to approach the mother about the fact that David's host family would like to adopt him. She was hard to gauge; one day she was thrilled, and the next day she was angry.

But we could not keep David in the states any longer. We would need to start the adoption process.

David came back to Honduras in 2012, after five years of living in the states. The adoption took two and a half years, and in 2014, David went home to Washington State and officially became David Bardal.

The church continued to grow and become a powerful positive force in our community. I don't think I have ever known how to do church "right" and our church always has been, and always will be, a little "off". We have struggled with all kinds of problems, and from the outside, it looks as if we are baby Christians. But let me tell you what happens on the inside: days of fasting, days of prayer and deep acts of selflessness. Each time a team was to come to Honduras to serve, we would have three days of prayer and fasting.

Prayer times were intense, and the youth were taught to deeply seek the Lord. Our prayer meeting nights are Thursdays, and they are something to experience! For someone like me who is at home around radicals, and these people are radical, it is my kind of spiritual home. We begin prayer each morning starting at 6:00 am. At least six to ten people are usually in attendance. We have seen many healings, deliverances and God shining through the hardships.

The church and the people of Honduras have taught me a lot about myself and humanity. They taught me what it really means to give in a way that pleases God. It is easy to show up in Honduras and wonder why the everyday Honduran does not do more for people who are in need. Many Hondurans feel that Hondurans are greedy. I see something quite different. Americans can be generous, but the truth is we give out of our wealth; Hondurans give out of their poverty. We give our leftovers, while Hondurans give their last or only. This was proven to me as I watched how they lived. The Honduran church purchased the land that the church, clinic and school now sit on. The truth is, that property was bought with blood, sweat and tears. Each month, to make the payments, the church had to work hard setting up food sale tents on the side of the road. Our church members sacrificed daily to make this dream a reality.

When we give, it usually means that we had enough to cover our own needs and wants, and only then do we give what is left over to someone who is truly in need. Hondurans literally give up something in order to give. Once I saw a situation where a father told his family they would only have milk that day, so they could give the other things in their pantry to people who had not eaten in many days. When I asked him why he was doing this, he said, "My kids ate yesterday, but their kids have not eaten in several days, and if not me, then who?" Such a profound question! Because he did not have excess, or a little for him and a little for others. He was sacrificing himself and his family. His options were, it's either you or me. And he decided, today it's going to be you, because I will do without. When the economy in the states had gotten bad and many sponsors contacted the ministry to let us know that they could no longer continue to send their donations, it was often Hondurans who stepped up and contributed when people in the US pulled out.

Hondurans in general have a concept regarding giving, and that is that you give your best, not your junk. Oscar has always taught our kids, if you have two pairs of jeans and you want to give one away to someone that needs them more than you, give them the best ones, not your garbage.

Hondurans rarely approach anything half-heartedly. They usually do things radically. Many times, our pastors work long, labor intensive, outside jobs, as well as work full time at the church. The workday in Honduras is typically 7:00 am to 5:00 pm, Monday through Saturday, and then spend all day serving in church on Sunday. In addition to home and hospital visits, they do prayer meetings, Bible studies, outreaches and all the other things that must be done in the evenings, after they get off their regular jobs. So, as you can imagine, they are not as "organized" as our American churches. But that is not to say that are not just as, if not more, power filled.

That year at the church, we started the Christmas basket program. Each year, in September, the church began doing major fund raising. The average income for most of our members' households is around $400-$600 per month. The idea for the event is that we dress to the nines; we invite the poorest families and make sure they have something nice to wear. The people that we invite usually live in extreme poverty, making as little as $20 a week for a family of five to nine people. We serve a wonderful Christmas dinner, and beautifully decorate the church. All the church members work extra jobs to get gifts for all the kids who will be coming, knowing that it will be the only gift they receive for Christmas. Then in addition, each guest family gets a basket to take home filled with a weeks' worth of food. Everyone participates and is thrilled to do it. One thing that is especially powerful in Honduras is when you show them they are not victims, and they actually become heroes.

I think it is a human need to give. It fulfills something inside us that nothing else can. Most Hondurans have been raised with a "victim" mentality. They firmly believe that they have nothing to give. However, when you show them how to do it, you have unleashed the kraken! Once they realize they can be givers, a new day has dawned for them, and they feel deeply empowered. Once this spirit was unleashed in our church, it became no-holds-barred.

We never "force" our kids at the Village to make any statement of faith, we simply live it before them, give them the truth and wait on the Lord to do the work in their hearts. Each Sunday our kids come into church and are taught with Sunday school materials generously donated by a church in Washington State. At the school, the children have a devotional each morning, where they experience worship and intercession. Our youth attend a dynamic youth group that includes outreach and local missions, as well as teaching them how to worship with passion and how to walk in the power of the Holy Spirit. We know that we could give them a home, an education, food and medical care, but what we can't do is heal and save their souls. For this, we have depended whole-heartedly on God alone. We learned years ago to leave the savior mentality at the door. We aren't the saviors; we need a Savior ourselves. But we know the One who is the Savior, and we do our best to point the kids to Him.

In 2007, thirteen of the kids we were raising asked to be

baptized. We generally don't baptize kids under twelve, and I think that year we baptized all but one child, twelve years and older. Honestly, this is my reward! I can't speak for any other person in H2H, but I am sure they would echo my thoughts; this is what it is all about. I often tell the kids, "Don't think I'm completely selfless; I do want a reward in all of this. And do you know what my reward will be? That each of you does well."

All of these kids were on a fast track to end up in jail, pregnant, in gangs or dead - but God! If the majority, or even just one can say, that because God recued me, I did not have that destiny handed to me, then all the work, all the sacrifice, and all the hardships are worth it. I firmly believe that if I was the only person on earth who needed salvation, Jesus would have come down and died for me. In H2H, we see each one as worth dying for! If just one in all of this ends up with a person who loves and respects them, enough money to cover their needs, and is healthy and happy, I will call that mission accomplished. However, they are exceeding my expectations. Once their ability to dream was turned back on, they were ready to turn the world upside down.

Many times, when we ask our kids what they want to do when they grow up, they are very resolved. "I want to give back what has been done for me, pay it forward." I often tell them, "We are nobody. Just some Americans who showed up, hoping to help where we could. But you are the ones who have been there." I want to see each of these kids grow up and go out into ministry work that will make ours look insignificant. We are the beginners, but they are the ones who will go out and reach Honduras and beyond, for Christ.

The Lord has always been so faithful to us. If the old saying goes, it takes a village to raise a child, then it takes a miracle to raise a village! The amount of resources you need to care for that number of kids is overwhelming. At this time in the ministry, we prayed for clean water. Our water source at the Village was either well water or city water, which were both unfit for drinking. Bottled water became expensive and boiling the water became tedious.

Once again, God had everything thought through. While Mary

was on one of our medical teams, she brought a group over to Roatán for some R &R. While she was on the beach, she heard two men talking about Jesus. So, she introduced herself to them. As it turned out, they were from Washington, Missouri and worked for a group called Washington Overseas Missions. They worked with water purification systems, which were exactly what we needed. So, with a grant from the Rotary Club, one year later, we had a water purification system put in at the Village. It purifies up to 500 gallons daily, more than enough to support our Village. Not only did they put the system in, they have also supplied us with the filters over the years.

Sometimes we face the need to make hard decisions, as every parent does. One factor that we have to deal with is we want to save kids who need help; however, we also have to protect the small children that we have. This may mean protection from the other older kids. In 2007, we had to ask a kid who had been with us from the beginning to leave. He was only fifteen, but it had become clear that he was not going to conform to our rules. We needed to release him back to the hard streets, in a hope to somehow save him. We will call him Tom.

He was one of the first five kids to live at the Village and had lived a full, hard life already by that time. He was nine years old at the time that he came and was living in a garbage dump at the local market. He had lived most of his life on the streets and had been the victim of a harsh stepfather. Honesty was difficult for him, and you could always count on Tom to cheat or lie somehow. Whenever there was a problem at the Village, the investigation usually uncovered that he was at the root of the problem. We dealt with him for years, but when it became clear that he was becoming a dangerous influence on the younger kids who feared him, we had to let him go. It was one of the hardest decisions that we have ever had to make. Tom went back to the streets to face its hard reality.

But that is not the end of the story, and we never meant it to be. Though we knew his problems, we really hoped that he would be able to turn his behavior around. Our ministry is all about second chances. The good news in this story is that he came back to us about one year later asking for forgiveness, and we did forgive him. He finished growing up at the Village, married his sweetheart from youth group at church and continues to serve in the church today with his wife.

As I said, and will repeat without ceasing throughout this book, God is faithful. He will always send you people for your life. In this case, He sent Dr. Nelly Hernandez. She was a local doctor we met when we brought a child into the hospital for treatment. She was curious and immediately fell in love with what we were doing. She pledged to come to the Village each Sunday to treat our kids medically. Throughout the years, she was a huge source of help when we needed someone at the hospital or clinic when our kids were sick or hurt. The year before, the nurse who had been serving at the Village had been sent to Roatán to work in a Hospital. Dr. Nelly was the person who helped us start our clinic in 2010, and then later worked for a short time in the clinic as our lead doctor.

In the summer of 2005, our family needed a break for personal reasons, and returned to the states for five months. When we returned to Honduras, we continued to take in children who were brought to our attention through people who knew of the ministry. One day, a set of pickup trucks from the government showed up at the Village. It was the Judge of the family court in San Pedro Sula and her posse. They had come to put us in our place, which basically meant to shut us down. They asked, "Where are your doctors and psychologists to help these children?" Oscar said, "Umm, no, we don't have any of that, but let me show you around."

Oscar began to show them the humble facility and introduce them to the kids. The judge was blown away with the quality of the food and the health of the kids. She asked how we kept the kids in without high walls. At first, Oscar really didn't even know what she was talking about. She explained to Oscar that all the public orphanages had ten-foot walls with razor wire on top of them to keep the kids from running away. Well, we didn't know anything about that. Our kids were happily at home. The judge told Oscar about conditions in the public orphanages, that the kids had only corn tortillas to eat. The group came with a mission to shut us down and left as new friends who offered their help in any way we needed. When Judge Antoinette left, she said, "Surely, this is a five-star children's home".

Oscar, however, was disturbed by the visit. He came home that night and said to me, "Amy, I swear I will not eat again until we get those kids at that orphanage some food!" In addition, when he told our kids at the Village the situation, they said without missing a beat, "Tío, we will eat one less tortilla each meal. We need to feed those kids at that orphanage!"

So, again, we called Mary and explained the situation to her. She suggested that she could send $400 for extra food right away, exactly the amount we had in mind! Then we purchased some bulk goods, such as beans, rice, grains, flour, diapers, with the funds that she sent. We loaded up the trailer that Oscar had built when we came to Honduras and headed out to the state-run orphanage.

I don't think I was ready for what I was about to see at that place. Children there suffered from the most awful effects of abandonment and neglect that you could imagine. Babies who did not cry, children who spent their entire day banging their heads against the walls and rocking themselves to sleep. Neglect and lack of love can kill, and this place was all the proof that you needed. We made our way up to the nursery where babies were "stored" two and three to a crib. When it was feeding time, the one worker who oversaw caring for about forty babies and toddlers, simply set their bottles in their mouths with a pillow. They were rarely held or taken out of their cribs, and most had pneumonia and horrible bed sores.

One of the littlest was a six-week-old baby they called China. I took her in my arms and would not put her down. I was remembering the time I visited the public hospital so many years before and wished I had done something. I thought to myself, this time, I'm doing something. I immediately changed her terribly soiled diaper and cut her extremely long fingernails. I fed her and rocked her all afternoon and told her, "China, you need a mommy." Oh, if I could have, I would have taken her home that day!

We took several people with us that day. Among them was Josué, who was one of our first five boys back in 2003. He was now sixteen and was about to have his life changed. Josué always loved small children and when we went up to the nursery, we also found "his" baby. It was a little girl who appeared to be about two years old. At first, she was shy, but after a while, her hunger for love and physical touch took over and she was in Josué's arms. One of the hardest things to do that day was leave. Josué suffered terribly when putting the little girl back in her crib. You could hear her cries from the hallway.

When we got back home, we all had to sit down and process the event. Oscar said that one of the biggest differences between our place and that orphanage was Jesus, and you could feel it! Josué swore if we went back for the little girl, he would take care of her! We did ask for them. We didn't have anything set up for a nursery, but I thought I could take China home. However, they told us that China and Josué's baby had been sent to another private children's home in La Ceiba, and I was happy for that.

It was also in this year that we met new friends stateside. Immanuel Lutheran Church of Centralia became a huge supporter of the ministry. As our family grew, the need to transport them all grew. At that time, we did not have a bus to get them to church; we were transporting them via several pickup trucks every week. The Immanuel Lutheran Church went right to work and got us a new seventy-two passenger bus.

That year, we also met Lisa and Scott Closner. Lisa was a drama teacher at Damascus Christian School in Oregon, who had come down with a team of her students to teach drama to our children. The kids learned skits that gave the message of salvation, and then they took them to the local villages and schools to present the skits. Lisa and Scott became friends of the ministry, serving on the board for a few years and bringing teams to help us. Lisa still serves as our sponsorship chairperson.

When we started WWH2H, we made tons of grand statements about who we were and what we did, and then God came along and said, "Why don't you let me decide?" Originally, on the wise counsel of another children's ministry who had twenty-five years of experience under their belt, we had decided that we would only be a home for boys between the ages of five and twelve. But then we realized that boys usually come with sisters, so we became a boys' and girls' home. Then we said, "Well, okay, we will have boys and girls, but we can't help handicapped kids because that would cost more than we can afford, both monetarily and with doctor care." Then David with his club foot and Cesar who was intellectually disabled came along. So, we said, "Well I guess we now have handicapped kids, God, but we cannot take babies. They require way more care that we can give them, lots of equipment and lots of money."

Mary was in Honduras when we got the phone call. We already had a child at the Village who was placed there, because she was being sexually abused by her father. The girl was nine years old and had Downs Syndrome. This time we were contacted by a social worker at the courthouse who told us there were actually seven other children in that family, and there was concern that the dad was abusing the other kids. The ages of the other children were: nine months, one and a half years old, three years old, four years

old, five years old, and ten years old. After picking them up, we took them back to the Village, fed them, and cleaned them up. Oscar was holding the nine-month-old and Mary had the one-and-a-half-year-old in her arms. He looked at Mary and said, "Well, Mary, are we opening our nursery?"

Within a few months, three more baby and toddler children joined our family, and we housed them temporarily in our former clinic building. By June of 2008, we had thirteen little ones.

As we grew in numbers, our kids also were growing up and some were becoming teenagers. We soon learned, that due to their history, they were prone to certain behaviors. The teen boys eventually came to Oscar and asked him to please get the teen girls away from them, because they were trying to be good boys. Apparently, the girls were aggressive sexually with the boys and the boys told us horror stories of what happened under the tables during meals. We knew that if we did not make a move to change that situation, we would end up creating new residents.

So, after much prayer and studying other organization that had been around longer than we had and had already crossed this bridge, we decide to rent a house in Puerto Cortes and move our teen girls out. We began right away to put a plan in place to build a girls' home.

Initially, we looked into buying another piece of property, but simply never found the land or the funding for the land. We put a fleece prayer out before the Lord, that if we did not find the land, we would simply build the Girls' House on the far end of our own property, with a dividing wall in between. When our deadline arrived, we realized that another property was not to be, and started construction on the back end of our eight-acre property. We had no funds but knew that it needed to happen. So, as we always do, we prayed, and the Lord brought us His funds.

A Mercy Ships team was in Honduras around that time, and a woman on the team became aware that we wanted to build a girls' home, but that we were without funds. As soon as she returned to the US, she called our headquarters and asked what our bank routing number was, because she wanted to send us some money. She deposited $20,000 into our account. In addition, many other people, who knew we were praying to receive the funds to build the house, began to send in donations toward the goal. In total, $70,000 was raised, and the girls' house was completed. They moved into their new home on January 1st, 2008.

Another great story revolving around the building of the girls' house was when we met Jim. Mary had spoken at her son's church in Addy, Washington, and many of the people from his church signed up to come on a team to work on the construction of the girls' house. One of those individuals was our soon-to-be-friend, Jim and his wife Tammy.

At the Seattle airport, as they were waiting to fly to Honduras, Jim, who is a formidable man, well over six feet tall, approached Mary shaking his finger in her face and said, "I just want you to know that the only reason I am on this team is because my wife made me come. I sat in that church service and heard you talk for an hour, all about the children and nothing about the bottom line. I just want you to know that I don't trust you, nor do I trust this ministry!" Mary simply smiled and said, "Okay Jim. I appreciate your honesty. Let's see what God has in mind."

Jim turned and walked away, as if he had not heard what she said, but Mary went right to prayer. When the team arrived, they began immediately on the projects, which were the electrical and plumbing work. Jim helped with the electrical, as he was a builder by trade.

Two boys from the Village, Nelson and Adonis who are brothers, attached to Jim right away. They always liked to take peoples' bandanas away, so he began calling them the "bandana banditos". You could see as he worked that he enjoyed the kids' help. Sometime during the middle of the trip, his wife approached us and said, "You won't believe what Jim suggested! He is concerned that you don't have the funds for the ceramic floor, so he wants us to purchase it, $5,000! Knowing how he felt about coming, I nearly fainted." She told us that the trip was deeply affecting his life.

Not only that, as the week went on, the couple fell more and more in love with the two boys and their older sister and even discussed trying to adopt them. Finally, the day came, and it was time for the team to leave. When they arrived back at the Seattle Airport and were getting ready to fly back to Spokane, Jim approached Mary one more time. This time with tears in his eyes, he gently put his arm around her and said, "Mary, I just want you to know something. I love you. I love these kids, and I love this ministry. My life has been changed forever, and I will never be the same!"

Jim was faithful with his promise and mailed a check to H2H for the Village. He also called Mary to let her know that he was the one to do the presentation about the trip at their church. He told her, "And guess who talked all about the kids and nothing about the bottom line?" Jim and Tammy continue to be beloved friends of the ministry.

On that same trip, Mary's son, Guy Bumstead, came to work on the Girls' House. Mary had told him about one of our girls who had come the year before. She was so terribly abused by the men in her family, that she did not even speak for almost two months. She spent much of her time crying, face turned to the wall, in her bed. Now, a year later, she was included in the birthday party celebrated by this team for the fourth quarter birthdays. We did not know her real birthday but wanted to include her. She had been following Guy around as he worked all week. When it came time for presents, she immediately got her gift sack and ran to Guy's lap to show him her treasures. He told Mary later, with tears in his eyes, that it was then that he realized she was the child that a year ago would not even speak, and here she was bonding with him, a man. She calls him her brother to this day and sings with him when he comes to help. They became a spiritual family.

One of the coolest stories from that year was about Hurricane Felix. Hurricane Felix was a category five hurricane that struck Honduras dead on but ended up being a total dud. All glory to God!

Eight years earlier, Honduras had been devastated by category five Hurricane Mitch, and much of the country was still reeling from that disaster. To this day, you can still see the effects of Mitch. Honduras is extremely poor, and the topography of the country does not handle big rain makers well. We heard that Felix was out in the Caribbean, and that it had its sights set on Honduras. We were concerned but went right to prayer. Mary sent a prayer request out to each person on our newsletter list asking for prayer. Many told me that they prayed throughout the night, and some said God had awakened them in the night to pray.

Before we went to bed the next night, it had been downgraded to a category one. Crisis averted, or so we thought. The next morning bright and early, we awoke expecting to find that it had fizzled out; however, to our horror, we discovered that overnight it had mushroomed into a monster! Now, a category five Hurricane again, with its sights still set on Honduras, we were in panic. We went into survival mode, battening down all the hatches, checking all the roofs and even discussing where we might evacuate the children should the situation become dangerous.

We called Mary right away, and she said that the prayers were still coming. We stayed connected to the news as it moved onto land near the Nicaraguan border. Within two hours, the storm had been downgraded to a category one hurricane, and by the afternoon it was only a tropical storm. By the evening, when it was over our area, it was a twenty-minute rain shower. As we watched the news, all the meteorologists were in shock. Felix went down in the record books as the fastest dissipating storm in history. In the end, there were no deaths due to Felix and only minimal damage. We call it praying down a storm, a testament to the power of prayer. It worked on Felix and has worked on every storm we have faced since.

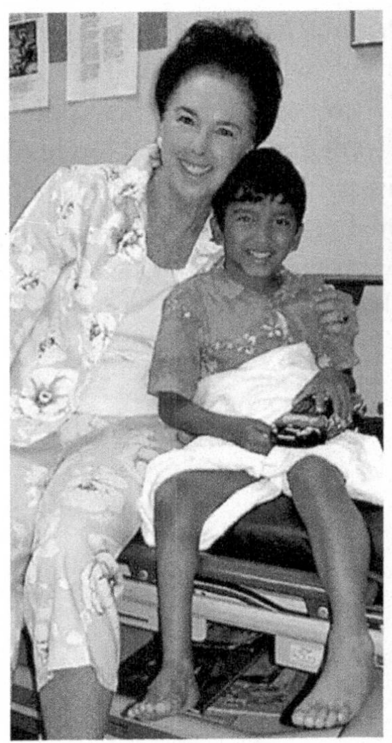

David Bardel and his family – also the Emmanuel Church

New Heart to Heart
medical clinic

The drama team, Lisa and Scott Closner, and Daniel Manzanarez

Visiting a public orphanage

Turcio family

Baby's house in Tegucigalpita

Building and cleaning the new girl's house at the Children's Village

Jim and the girls from the Children's Village

Centralia team

12

Growing God's Way

"Therefore I say unto you, Take no thought for your life, what ye shall eat, or what ye shall drink; nor yet for your body, what ye shall put on. Is not the life more than meat, and the body than raiment? Behold the fowls of the air: for they sow not, neither do they reap, nor gather into barns; yet your heavenly Father feedeth them. Are ye not much better than they?"
(Matthew 6: 25-26)

It was now 2008, and we were celebrating our fifth year of rescuing children. Each day we were moving along and getting stronger and helping more people. That year we purchased a piece of property, where the church built a new building. The owner of the property was a Christian woman who sold it to us for a third of its market value. It came with a few partially completed buildings already on it which worked well as the foundations of the buildings that we wanted to build.

We also realized that we now were up to fifteen baby and toddler children, and the three-bedroom home that they were in was not going to be sufficient. We began to pray and knew that our next move was to build a proper home for them. We decided that we would build it next to the girls' house at the other end of the property. So yet again, we picked up shovels and began to break ground without a penny in hand. But we did as we always do, we went to the Lord in prayer.

It was a Friday in early August 2008 that Oscar called Mary and said he needed funds to build the Baby House. They prayed. Two days later, Mary was speaking at the local Carson Nazarene Church about Honduras. After the service, a couple and their grandson came up to her. The man said, "Do you believe in Divine Appointments?" She said she did. He told her this was one of them. He said he was Paul Chiles and this was his wife, Joyce and their grandson, Lauren. They were visitors to the church that day. They had a summer home on the nearby Columbia River and had decided to find a local church to attend that morning, as they waited for family to arrive for a picnic.

As they listened to Mary speak during the church service, their grandson turned to his grandpa and said, "That lady was my first-grade teacher!" Lauren had been adopted from Romania years before by their son and daughter-in- law and had been placed in Mary's first grade class at Stevenson Elementary for the two months they lived there. Now, here he was, a teenager, coming to church with his grandparents! Paul told Mary he and his wife worked on first responder teams all over the world for Samaritan's Purse, a Franklin Graham ministry.

They had been in Honduras for a year after Hurricane Mitch and knew all the places Mary had been speaking about. Paul asked her what she needed. She told him funds to build a Baby House. He told her to make a one-page proposal for the Baby House and send it to him. The very next day, as Mary opened her computer to begin the proposal, Paul had already emailed her and said, please send me the proposal. I am serious about this. Mary promptly wrote up the proposal and sent it to him. Within days the response came. Samaritans Purse would give us $25,000 toward the construction of the Baby House she and Oscar had just prayed about a few days before!

The work went forward, and much was done with that money. The foundation was poured, walls started going up and the work progressed with great joy. Teams came down and helped with different aspects of the construction. But the day finally came in the spring of 2009, when the funds ran out. Oscar called Mary on a Sunday in April and told her that they were out of funds and that, if there were no more funds available to send, he would go ahead and tell the men that the construction project was on hiatus until further notice. Mary told him she had $500 she could send. Oscar said that would keep the construction team working for a week. They prayed.

Two days later, Mary was at a friend's house planning the V.B.S. team that would come in November. During the meeting, she received a phone call from Scott Closner, one of our board members. Scott told her that one of his friends had written a bestselling book and wanted to send H2H a donation and needed our ministry address. She told Scott this was a direct answer to the prayer she and Oscar had just prayed two days before, for funds to keep the Baby House construction going. "Do you have any idea how much he is going to send?" Scott asked Mary. Mary guessed about a couple thousand dollars. Scott replied, "He is sending you $50,000!" We were blown away, to say the least! The construction was not going to be put on hold. It was enough to get our Baby House finished and then some.

One great reality is that many of the children were already in our custody when these homes were built. We did not build them and then look for the kids. When a child in need came along, we took them in and trusted God to provide for their needs. In the end, He always proved Himself true. He had it all worked out!

By this time, we had built our Boys' Home, our Girls' Home, our Baby House and the church. Life was going well. Josué, one of our first five boys, had big news that year; he was getting married!

When we met Josué, he was living under a bridge in Puerto Cortes. His mother was deaf, and his father had never been part of his life. Josué was one-too-many mouths for his poor disabled mother to try and feed, so he was pushed out of the house. He was eight years old when he went to try to find a life with his aunt who lived in town. She took him in, but only in order to make him a slave to her other children. Josué was not put in school, but rather was made to serve his cousins and was beaten and treated harshly by his aunt. At thirteen, he had had enough, and decided to try to make it on the streets. Living under a bridge can be very dangerous. Predators, in particular, look for young boys who are on their own. He started asking the local fishermen if he could help them clean the fish for a little bit of food.

When we found Josué, we asked him if he would like to live and work at the Village; he came that same day. I can honestly say that these first boys who came, truly helped us build all that you see at the Children's Village in Tegucigalpita. Josué went to school. Though he was only scholastically at a second-grade level, he excelled and did well. He joined the youth group at our church and ran the library. When he was sixteen years old, he started dating Cesia, and two years later the two married. The next year they had their first child, our first grandbaby! Two years later, their second child, a son, was born. Today, Josué is our Village Manager. His daughter is in second grade and his son is in Prepa at our Christian Bilingual School.

This was also the year that we got the Hernandez family. Our friend Allison called us one day and told us that she had been contacted by the hospital and told that there was a critically ill child there, who would need a home and someone to care for her. It turned out the child, in the last critical stages of starvation, was not the only child in the family. One other child from that family had already died from complications due to starvation. Allison stayed with the girl in the hospital for over a week, and finally, she came back around and survived. She came to live with Allison and began to thrive. Several months later, we got a phone call from a social worker at the courthouse. They told us that there was a situation in a family with many children who were suffering from severe malnutrition, and one child in the family had already died.

When I heard that the child had died, it made me curious to know if this family could be the same family that the child with Allison had come from. We went with a person from the courthouse to visit the family. To get to this family's home, we had to drive an hour away, then hike up into the Honduran jungle for at least another hour. They lived in a village that was extremely poor and the parents happened to be the village pastors.

When we walked into the home, we found a three-year-old child standing alone in the middle of the kitchen holding a large seed in his hand. He would not talk to us, nor would he move. His legs and arms were very skinny, but his belly and cheeks were huge, sure signs of malnutrition. The home was extremely humble. The floor was just dirt, and the walls were simply sticks that were planted in the ground with palm branches for a roof. On the stove, not far away, was a boiling pot, so we knew that adults had to be close. Within a few minutes, a group of teenage kids arrived with some younger children. They were the siblings of the child in the home. I looked into the pot and saw three or four green bananas boiling and asked them what they were making. They told me the bananas were all they had, and what was in that pot would be dinner for nine people.

After a few questions to the siblings, my suspicions were confirmed; they were indeed the same family as the child living with Allison. The social worker that we were with did not have a court order to take the children, but rather hoped that we could talk to the parents and see if they would be willing to turn their kids over to us. Since they were not home, the social worker told the older kids to let them know that we would come back the next day.

When we arrived the next day, the parents were indeed home, and not that impressed that we wanted to take their children. Oscar sat with the man and told him that his other children were also on the verge of death, if they did not receive better sanitation, nutrition and care. The father finally admitted that he could not care for them and agreed that the kids could come with us. Oscar, the father and the social worker gathered all the kids together, and then the unexpected happened. As if the kids already knew and had it planned, they each ran up into the mountains in a different direction. Oscar, the social work and Marvin, who was with him, ran after them and trekked through the jungle for more than an hour. After giving up, they returned to the home and found that all the kids had returned and were ready to leave with them.

Today their sister still lives with Allison and is a beautiful, healthy girl. The oldest girl is still at our Village is now eighteen and is doing well. The seventeen, fourteen, ten and eight-year-old brothers are also thriving! The children's parents often come to visit them at church.

We continued to receive teams which came to perform many different important functions for us. Almost all went very well, but then there were one or two that were really strange. One was a medical team that we had that year.

Two or three years earlier, I had an interesting conversation with Allison Alexander. Before she came to the north coast to start her own ministry, she had worked with another ministry near the capital city of Tegucigalpa. She told me a horror story about a man who had come to work at that ministry and had kidnapped two girls from the children's home and had been found in a hotel with them and was arrested. I, of course, was horrified! The thought ran through my head, "Oh, Lord; please don't ever let that man come near our Village."

In 2008, we had a medical team coming from the Pacific Northwest and the director told me that one of their team members was already in Honduras and had been doing dentistry with another group in Tegucigalpa. He was going to be meeting up with the team in Cortes and was being driven by a friend. When they arrived, I spoke with the man who was the driver, an American. I mentioned that some of our other translators were from a children's home in Tegucigalpa and he was immediately very excited. As it turns out, he had been a volunteer at that same children's home. As the ministry is very large and hosts thousands of volunteers, I was excited to see that we had some commonality.

I did get his name and asked Allison if she knew him. Her girls were going to be helping us the next day with translation. She said she did know him; his name was Antonio (not his real name). I asked her if he was all right, because he would be around our kids all week, and she told me that he was fine. Apparently, she said that he and his whole family had gone down to Honduras to help at the children's home, but then his wife left him. He stayed and worked a few more years at the home. So, the medical team began, and all was going well. Allison's girls came to translate and were very excited to see Antonio.

Antonio seemed to be very well behaved; however, the doctor he was translating for was horrible. He was screaming at the children and was throwing his medical instruments around when he was angry. Some of the older girls told us that he told them that he was a "dirty old man". We were very concerned, but the director of the team told us that he would take care of it. One or two days before the team visit was over, Allison, came over to our house, notably upset. She said that her girls would not be going the next day to translate. It appears that the man translating was not who she thought he was, as she had never really met him. She said his name is not Antonio, its Tony, the very same man that had been arrested in the hotel!

When she said that, my hands went numb, my knees were weak, and I could hardly breathe. The thing that I had most feared was now upon me! Immediately, we went to the hotel to tell them that they could no longer go to the Village or be around the kids. It appears we just missed them. When the director of the team confronted the doctor about his behavior, he got angry and decided to leave with his friend, also known as my worst nightmare! The most interesting thing about all this is that though he had been arrested in Honduras, he had no criminal history in the United States. We know, because all volunteers who work at our Village must submit to a background check. Today H2H has a very strict background check policy. If you volunteer with H2H, please understand why.

Some teams, however, were downright hysterical. One team that was great, was a team lead by Lisa Closner and Ashley Kwasney. Ashley, from Montana, had been on the very first team that had come to Honduras back in 2000. This time she and Lisa had both come with their respective youth groups from their churches and had a plan. It was spring break and we were going to send the house mommies home for a few days and take care of all the kids ourselves.

To say the resulting situation was chaos would be an understatement! They acquired an extremely healthy respect for all that our mommies do every day, as they managed the schedule for all the kids for just a few days. One of the days they were there, we decided to drive into San Pedro Sula and take the kids out to a movie and lunch.

Honduras, just as many very poor countries, suffers from two extremes; the very poor, and the "how-could-you-live-here-with-so-much-money" type. The industrial capital of Honduras, San Pedro Sula, can offer you both, deep poverty, but also pockets that look as if they could belong to wealthy Americans. The mall is a good example. When you step in, you see many familiar stores and restaurants that are American chains. The polished marble floors and high ceilings resemble a mall in the United States, and not just any mall, but a more upscale mall. Since this is where the movie theater is located, this is where we took the kids to have their first real movie experience.

Just before that, we took the kids to Pizza Hut for lunch. Pizza is a strange food to the kids. It seems that it is a little like opera, either you love it or you hate it. The Pizza Hut in San Pedro Sula, however, offers a huge playland where all the kids could have the time of their lives. As the kids were playing, one of our older girls came down the slide with her hands covered in blood. It looked like a scene from a horror movie. We asked her what had happened, but she said that the blood was not hers, it was on the playground. Oscar kicked his shoes off and ran into the play structure looking for who was hurt. We went kid by kid asking who had been hurt, and all said that it was not them. As our kids were not the only kids in the play area, we finally assumed that it someone else's kid. We called the staff at the restaurant, and they came and cleaned the mess.

As we were all sitting down to eat, I noticed that Nelson, sipping on his pop, had a huge stream of blood going down his forehead and dripping off his nose. He seemed none the worse for wear, as if it didn't even bother him. We called him over and apparently, he had not even noticed. He told us that he had stood up in the play structure and that there was a screw sticking down from the top of the structure. When he stood up, it stabbed him in the top of his head. We treated his injury right away and finally were on our way to the movie.

I think we take a lot of life in western civilization for granted. Many of us grew up in cities and have been to malls since early childhood, so something like an escalator is very normal. To these kids the "moving stairs" were something they wanted nothing to do with! Getting them to get on the escalator was quite a challenge; however, once we did, the escalator was a bigger hit than the movie! The bathroom was on the second floor, and the movie theatre was on the third floor. Curiously enough, the kids needed to go to the bathroom frequently, so that they could ride the escalator of course! We took the kids to the movie "Horton Hears a Who", which they thoroughly loved, and then made our way back to the Village. Yet another new experience for the kids, and lots of learning for us.

To be a parent, as many of you know, often requires great creativity. Such was the case with Adonis. He was seven years old and apparently had a bad tooth. The night before, he had been up all night struggling with the pain. The next day we took him to the local dentist. There are no words to adequately express what this dentist office looked like. It had a dirt floor and the dental chair appeared to be an electric chair, as there were straps attached to tie you in, if they were needed.

Adonis allowed the dentist to give him the injections to numb his mouth. But when the dentist approached with the pliers to pull out the tooth, Adonis was not having it! He absolutely refused, with tears and screams. I did all that I could. I said, "Come on Adonis, we are going to do it now, one, two three." But nothing worked. We tried and tried to convince him, but to no avail. The dentist told me that soon the Novocain would be wearing off, and we needed to decide. I called Oscar on the phone and told him that I didn't really know what to do. I thought that perhaps I could try it again the next day, but that would mean that Adonis would again have a difficult night.

Oscar asked me to pass the phone to Adonis, and he talked to him. Adonis put the phone to his ear and huffed and puffed, through his tears. He whined, but through his tears I could hear him say, "sí, huff puff, sí." Then he handed the phone back to me, and I began to walk out of the room telling Oscar that we would try again tomorrow, when I heard cheering behind me. To my amazement, Adonis was in the chair and the dentist was standing over him with the tooth in his pliers. I still had Oscar on the phone, so asked him,

"Oscar what did you tell him?" I was very confused because I had just spent the last thirty minutes pulling out all the "kid" techniques I knew. And Oscar just talks to him for a few moments and the tooth is out. What's up with that? Oscar said, "Well, I told him that now that the injections had been put in, if he did not let them remove the tooth, his head might fall off." Never a dull moment.

As we continued to work at pushing forward, bringing in more kids and helping as many as we could, more people within Honduras began to become aware of us. One of our Honduran board members was related to a Mayor in a town about three hours away and had been telling him what we were doing. He immediately wanted to meet with us. We went to his beautiful mountain village that was high in the coffee country of Honduras. The name of the town was Concepción Del Sur. The mayor told us that he wanted to offer us something like what we had already done in Cortes. He wanted to donate land in their village and asked us to develop another children's village like we had in Tegucigalpita. We again did not have funds but accepted happily. We told them that we could do nothing at that moment, but that as soon as God provided the funds, we would start right away. We thought it may be a matter of months, but we were not able to start anything there until 2015.

On a sad personal note, in 2008 I lost two people very dear to me. My dad died on September 28th, Oscar's birthday, and my great aunt also died that year. Both left us an inheritance. With it, my dad made a special request before he died that we build a home in Honduras with the money. So, with the funds in hand, we began the construction of our own home in Honduras. Until that time, we had either lived with friends or rented.

All was well and children were being restored. We were overjoyed at all that the Lord had done so far. Little did we know that something big, destructive and overwhelming was about to knock on our door. It almost took us out - but God! It was the economic recession of 2008 and the Honduran political coup of 2009.

Oscar and author Paul Young

Lisa and Scott Closner emceeing one of the H2H annual banquets

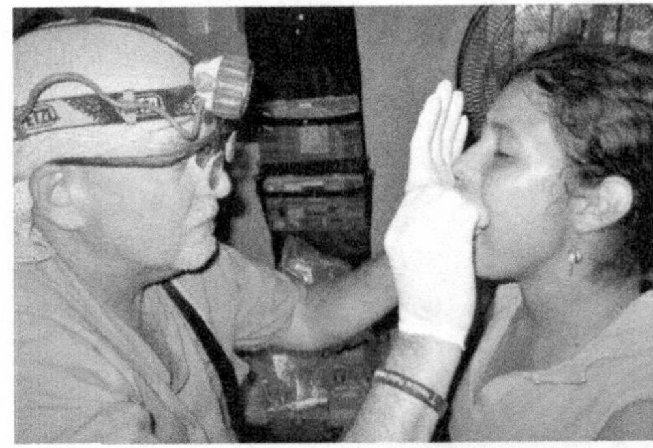

Dr. Bill Mays with Medical Relief International

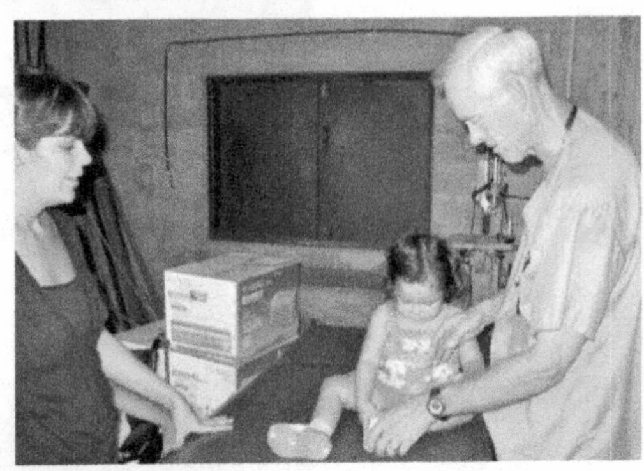

Alison, Araceli and BobTutland

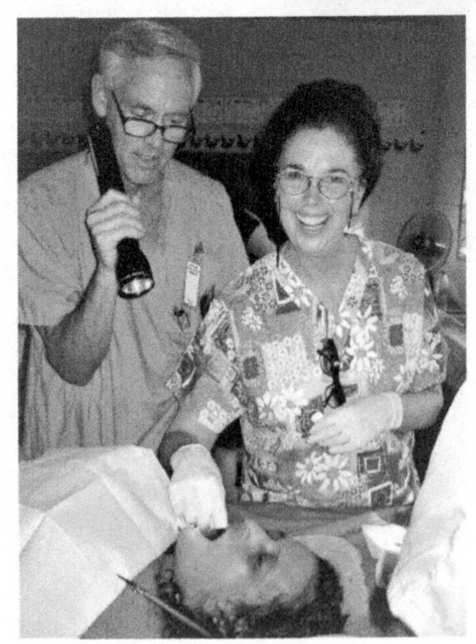

Mary and her brother, Bob Tutland

Denia

Keren Hernandez

Daniel Hernandez

Alberto and Nahun Hernandez

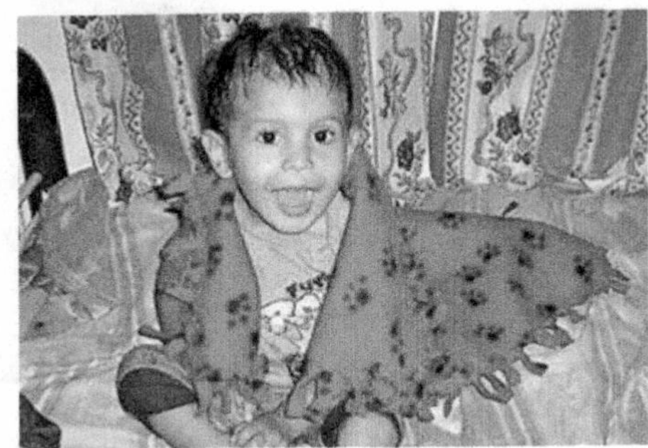

Kevin Hernandez

Adonis and Nelson Barias

Amy and her dad Isidore Rills with daughters Sarah and Rachel

13

A Year of Famine

"He that dwelleth in the secret place of the Most High shall abide under the shadow of the Almighty. I will say of the Lord, He is my refuge and my fortress: my God; in him will I trust."
(Psalm 91:1-2)

The year 2009 started just like every year. We were excited for what the New Year held, and we had lots of dreams and plans. Each day, we wanted to help more children come off the streets. A new president had just been elected in Honduras. His name was Mel Zelaya. He was a relative newcomer to the political scene; however, he did spend some time as the country's project development manager. Thankfully, he was not one of the "good ol' boys" of the Honduran political scene.

Wil and Jane Meckle, US board members, started a "Christmas in July" program that year. It was a large benefit dinner that was done at their church to raise funds and collect Christmas presents for the kids. Lisa Closner started the letter writing teams which came down and helped the kids write to their sponsors, and a gracious donor from New Mexico, Grant Kolb, began to send us books in Spanish to build a library. All was going splendidly, and then things started to go downhill.

Sometimes our hearts are bigger than our reach. If there has been anything that we have been accused of, it is that we bite off more than we can chew, a fault we definitely had that year. We had been visiting the public orphanage in San Pedro Sula for many years. There was not much that you can say about that place. Often the nursery consisted of two to three babies per crib. They often get on their hands and knees and rock themselves, hitting their heads on the crib bars.

They do this because they are never held or touched, and it is their form of stimulation. There were also handicapped children who were tied down to their beds because there was not enough staff to care for them and protect them. The girls were put into the craft room and locked in, for two reasons. First, it kept them from the boys, and second, it kept the workers from abusing them. But it didn't work. When we first went to visit the public orphanage in San Pedro Sula, we were invited there by the judges who had come to visit us.

Now, we frequently visited the orphanage and saw the need and were doing all that we could to help. The director of the orphanage told us that the orphanage was never meant to be a home to the kids there, but rather a transition place before they were sent to a private orphanage, as soon as space became available. We made a bold decision that year to do our best to help the orphanage accomplish that. We decided that since we had room for nineteen more children at the Village, we would take nineteen children from the orphanage to live there.

Building community is a fragile thing, but even more so with the damaged personalities that come with abandoned and abused children. A community of children has a certain PH balance. When we took in our first five kids, we had lots of one on one time with them and were able to disciple them more intensely. Then, as we added children, one by one or two by two, those children naturally acclimated to the routine that existed at the children's home. When we took in the new nineteen children, many of whom had just recently been living on the streets, it changed the atmosphere of the Village in a negative direction.

The new kids made up about 30% of our total residency. Instead of the kids who had already been "rehabilitated" changing the new kids who came in, the new kids were changing the kids who were already in the Village. Behavior problems mounted and we had to do double time to really focus on our new kids' discipline and counseling. Half of the new kids ran away in the first three months. Within the year, another five or six ran away.

We realized that we had become the victim of the thing we had tried never to have, "Savior Complex"! We were sure that we would come in and be the "solution" for that terrible orphanage in San Pedro Sula, and then we were put in our place. I always tell people when I teach on missions, the two greatest temptations for a missionary are not sex, money or power, but rather the temptation to look at a need, know you need to respond, or at least think that you know, but say, no I really can't! That is too hard! After all, doesn't the Bible say if you know what is right to do and you don't do it, that is sin? We really thought that, even though it would be hard, we could do it, but the reality was we couldn't.

That decision, once taken, took years to right itself with deep prayer and hard work. We are thankful for the nine of the nineteen children who did stay. Jairo, Blanca, Lesley, Luis, Julio, Nicole, Corbin, Karla and Kevin are worth all the sacrifice in the world.

One of the young girls who came with that group was a girl named Joy (not her real name). She had been so severely abused by her drunken father, that she was now crippled. He had broken her hips and pelvis in eight places, and she was now living with chronic infections and could no longer walk. The abuse that this poor child had suffered was horrific.

That abuse however, caused wounds far deeper than her hips. Greater still were the tremendous emotional wounds that had been inflicted on her deeply scarred heart and spirit. Joy did well at the Village for a few weeks in the beginning, but then began to display severe behavior issues. She was unstoppable and rebellious in her behavior toward the housemothers. But even worse, she was violent with the other kids. We immediately went straight to two things, prayer and spiritual intervention in her life, and counseling with a professional psychologist.

I brought Joy to a private room and explained to her that certain things open doors in the spiritual realm and give authority to Satan in our lives. Joy and I prayed, and I had Joy repeat after me, renouncing the witchcraft that had been in her family and all the spiritual baggage that she was carrying. After praying with her that day, she confessed with her lips that Jesus was Lord of her life, and I believed that she was 100% born again. We had a beautiful time of singing, crying and praying.

But Joy was on a journey. The fact is, I was reluctant to even put Joy's story in this book. Remember, I told you that H2H was about to experience some hard times. It was not just financial or political, it was also spiritual. Joy's story does not end well. Even after the prayer and spiritual intervention, Joy was struggling immensely with her behavior and emotional outbursts. We took her to a Christian psychologist, who immediately put her on medications and treated her for emotional disorders. The psychologist told us from the beginning that she was deeply concerned about Joy, and that she displayed suicidal, as well as homicidal tendencies.

At the Village we kept Joy closely monitored, as well as continued in prayer for healing, both physically and spiritually. But there was only so much that we could do. One day the levy broke. One other little girl who was in the same room with Joy, had received a beautiful new dress for her birthday from her sponsors who were in Honduras on a mission team. I am assuming that it was jealousy or just general unbridled rage that took over Joy, but while all the kids were out of the room, Joy took a pair of scissors and cut the little girl's new dress into pieces. Another little girl had come into the room and saw what was going on and immediately ran out of the room to find the owner of the dress. She ran into the room in tears gathering the shredded pieces in her hands, as Joy stood back laughing.

The little girl screamed at Joy and said, "Why did you do this to me?" Joy, in response, with scissors still in hand, decided to use the scissors on her. Though she could not walk, she scooted on her bottom across the room, scissors in hand and began to lash out at the little girl. The house mommies ran into the room and it required three of them to get Joy off the bleeding little girl. By the grace of God, the little girl only suffered minimal surface wounds; however,

Joy was out of control. One of the house mommies noticed Joy had tried to discreetly push the scissors under the bed. The psychologist told us that unfortunately, she probably meant to hide them for later; once everyone had gone to sleep, she would finish off the little girl.

The concern was that now this was not just a fit of anger, it was premeditated. She was planning how to hurt, how to kill! The little girl's sponsors were irate! They demanded that we send Joy somewhere else immediately, or they would go and tell other sponsors what was "really happening" at H2H. We were very concerned. Joy was targeting other children smaller than herself with intentions of doing great physical harm to them. We needed to protect Joy, but we needed to protect the others as well.

We began to pray and again the next day we received a call from the Village that one of the house mommies had quit. She could not deal with Joy, and other house mothers threatened to do the same thing. We could honestly say that at that time, we had done all we knew how to do. We had had the entire church and other Christian brothers and sisters with gifts of deliverance, pray over her and anoint her with oil. We had taken her to the psychologist and had her in therapy and on medication. At this point, we felt that we needed to protect the other children at the Village, and that we could not do anything more to help Joy. With deep sadness, we had to return Joy to a state institution. However, I am pleased to say that before she left, we were able to get her the surgeries she needed, and she was able to walk with the assistance of a cane. We did follow her over the years. She went to another home and stayed there until she was eighteen. She now lives with her family in Copan, Honduras.

In December 2009, we were able to do something fun with all our children, before some began to run away. That year instead of having their new Christmas outfits purchased in the US, we decided that it would be fun to take all the children on a shopping spree. We first took them to a restaurant in town for lunch and then on to the shops. It was virtually impossible to do this in one trip, so we decided to do boys first and then girls. It was again just north of total chaos, but it was so nice to see the kids get to do normal stuff!

One thing that we strive to do here, is to make their lives as "non-institutional" as possible. Many people who come alongside us want to complicate the kids' lives saying, "To maintain order here, there needs to be a schedule! This schedule should outline the day from the time they wake up, to the time they go to bed." I really don't know about you, but I don't think our family had a schedule growing up. Sure, I had to wake up at 6:00 am each morning in order to go to school. I would return from school and dinner was usually sometime between 5:00 and 6:00 pm. I always had to get showered before bed and get my homework and chores done, but I don't remember having a schedule. There was family time, time to watch TV with the family or have free play with our toys, but never a rigid schedule. So, why do they think a schedule would cause a child to be normal?

Since some of the kids that we brought shopping were from the public orphanage, we did have one incident. The girls had just finished their shopping and were getting on the bus, when one of the employees said that they thought that perhaps one of the girls may have items in her bag she did not "purchase". With great embarrassment, I asked the older girls on the bus to help me figure out who it might be, and that did not take long. One of the older girls found a few pieces of jewelry and some makeup in the bag of one of the younger girls. I was so sad! When we had arrived at the store, all the attendants were so excited to help all of these underprivileged kids shop for clothes! Now, as I walked back into the store, totally ashamed, with the stolen merchandise in hand, everyone looked at me with the "what kind of mother are you" face.

With a portion of the inheritance funds I had received the year before in 2008, we decided to build our house, and it was well underway. We had decided that we would build a hotel-type home that we would live in and manage. Up to that point, we were hosting up to thirty teams per year. Each of those teams had to pay for a hotel, which could add up to thousands of dollars each year. We thought that it would be a good idea to find a way to put that huge investment in lodging costs toward helping the kids instead. We would open the house and charge team members the same fees to stay with us, but the proceeds would go back to the kids.

However, something began to become abundantly clear, and we felt the Lord had begun to shift us in another direction. As I already mentioned, 2009 through 2011 were very hard years for us, personally as well as for H2H as a whole. A couple of our now teenaged girls at the Village, began to run away. They ran off with men much older than themselves and were pregnant within months of leaving. Subsequently, the men that they ran away with abandoned them as soon as they became pregnant. We were having a great crisis with our girls. We were at the Village each day anointing the whole property with oil, praying over the girls, praying over the house mommies, sitting with girls and talking things out. We did book studies with the girls, but the situation was going from bad to worse. My spiritual arms and hands grew weak; I couldn't do it anymore and gave up. We had prayer meetings at our church on Thursday nights, and as I sat with my prayer group that night, I complained and heaped sorrow on myself regarding the situation. I told the ladies I was praying with, that I was done; I had given up on the girls.

At that time, our future pastor's wife, Rosa Castro, stood up and said, "Amy, you are the anointed mom in that house! You don't let the devil tell you how it is going to be, you tell him how it is going to be!" That was just the slap in the face that I needed. I was immediately ashamed of my behavior and repented before the Lord. The next day I went out to the Village and gathered the girls' house mothers, who were also at their wits end and ready to throw in the towel. I told them, "Ladies, the devil has had his way far too long! We are going to start taking back territory right now!"

We whipped out the anointing oil and walked throughout the Village, anointing the whole property, taking it back in the name of Jesus. I prayed over each woman and asked the Lord for wisdom on how to minister to the girls. First, I had to ask for their forgiveness for nearly giving up on them. Second, we all stood in a circle holding hands and prayed for the Lord's presence to fall on us. We prayed and sang, and you could feel the spirit of funk breaking off and little girls coming out of the cloud. The Lord gave me ideas of how to minister to them in smaller groups, and that seemed to be received better.

It did not happen overnight, but within a few months of great persistence, the girl's house once again became a place of tranquility. The girls returned to simple obedience and were much more at peace.

We felt that the teenaged girls now needed a discipleship program, just as our boys had. After praying intensely, we knew that God wanted us to use our home for the teen girl discipleship program and that Oscar and I needed to run it. Today we have eighteen girls who live in our home with our own two teenaged daughters, Sarah and Rachel.

With another portion of the inheritance funds that we had received, we decided to establish a way for the girls to learn a trade. We traveled to the states and purchased all necessary items needed to start a beauty salon college. We hired our son Josué's new wife, Cesia, to run the college, as she was a beautician. Within two years, our first five girls had become licensed beauticians. We also tried to start a coffee shop and souvenir business to help the ministry, but soon discovered that we were way too busy at that time to try anything like that and decided to close them down.

In 2009, a wonderful man from New Mexico by the name of Grant Kolb, a US Geologist, began to help us. He called our President, Mary Frenter, one day in February and told her he found our web page online and had been reading it and weeping for two days. He wanted to know how he could help. She told him we needed books for a library for the kids. Grant began to send us brand new books in Spanish that were great for the kids. They were often the classics, like *Tom Sawyer*, *Don Quixote*, and *Little Women*. We set up an entire room at the Village and had shelves built that became the Village Library. This was especially great for Mary, who was a teacher for thirty-six years and had dreamed for years of having a library for the kids. Over the years, Grant has supplied many more books, puppets, and shoes and other needs for the children.

It was May of that year and tensions were high, politically! The two major political parties in Honduras were becoming more and more polarized, and the president was becoming more and more of a leftist, rubbing elbows with the presidents of the socialist countries in South America.

We had a medical team planned that year which started out as a rather large team, but one by one, with the political situation in Honduras becoming more and more unstable, team members began to drop off. Then within just weeks of a departure date, Mary called us to say that this once mighty team was now down to only five members. She wondered if they should even bother coming at all. We, however, really believed this may be the hand of God.

Ever since Marvin came to live at the Village, we had had a great heart and a calling to his village of Las Flores. We had always wanted to take a medical team there, but there were a few obstacles. Number one, you practically needed a hover craft to get up there. At certain times of the year, the roads were completely impassable. In addition, it was a very small village, perhaps a few hundred people, and no "gringo" accommodations at all. A large medical team simply would not work, however, a small one would.

We asked the five remaining ladies on the team if they were up for the challenge and all were very excited. In addition, Allison Alexander of Eternal Family Project ministry had some visiting team members who asked if they could tag along and help with translating and logistics. The team made their way to Las Flores to do four days of medical missions.

This is the story told by one of the doctors who lived it!

That Fateful Day in Honduras

By Allison Mattila

The Medical Group serving in Honduras in late May 2009 had some amazing adventures. I am a Family Nurse Practitioner from a Federally Funded Health Center and this was my third mission into the country and the first time traveling without a dental team, a medical doctor, or a large support group. The five of us traveling met during the trip down. I was the first to arrive, followed by Joanie the team Mom, Diane the emergency/surgical nurse, and Robyn the pharmacy technician. We met

Amy, a pharmacy representative from Illinois, during the connecting flight in Houston. Each of us knew maybe one or two other team members when we started the trip and little did we know that we would be sharing an experience that would bind us together for a lifetime.

After spending the first day at the Children's Village and meeting our fellow in-country team members, the group took the five-hour truck journey into Las Flores to serve the people living in the nearby villages. None of us knew what to expect for sleeping, showering, or clinic set up. When we arrived at the school, we chose classrooms to use as bedrooms, storage, medical clinic, craft distribution, and (most importantly) the kitchen. Our fellow team members, Oscar Serrano, Oscar Vasquez, Cristelia, Eliny, Marcel, and Miguel all set up their areas.

Clinic days were hectic, hot and humid beyond belief. There was a huge learning curve for all of us. We had to set up medications, organize our "exam areas", and make sure everyone had a job. Diane was thrown into the role of "doctor" right away to service the volume of patients. Robyn had to organize and distribute medications with instructions written in Spanish. Amy learned medication dosage and routes on the job, and Joanie worked hard to oversee it all. As the only member from a previous group aside from Joanie, I assisted everyone in set up and worked with Joanie to organize the flow. Marcel manned the door, the women prepared the kitchen, and Miguel and the Oscars handled crowd control. We also had with us Stacey, Kara, Cynthia, and Abby (the "Tennessee Girls") to help with blood pressures, organize craft activities, and teach the children about the gospel.

Despite some hitches along the way, the clinics flowed well. We were able to see everyone who came to us for care and help. Some walked more than 4 hours to see us in high temperatures and humidity. Patients were seen for headaches, infections, body pains, fevers, allergies, rashes, and other ailments. Some of the people we saw had never seen a medical provider in their lifetime! Even a few of the team members had illnesses or ailments that everyone worked together to help with. We experienced the first earthquake Honduras had had in the last decade and had a ton of fun.

After clinics ended for the day, we would go to the river to cool off and shower. I discovered the joy of bathing in a natural sulfur spring and exfoliating with river mud and others enjoyed the massage of sitting in the rapids. We all teased and joked like the family we were rapidly becoming. After the river, we would return to the clinic for dinner and a movie. The "screen" was a white sheet tacked onto the wall of the school, and Oscar Serrano set up his computer to play through a projector and a large speaker. It seemed as if the whole town came out to watch Wall-E, and Kung Fu Panda! After the movie, there was down time where we would watch the fireflies, listen to the Tennessee Girls sing amazingly well, and talk about the day.

The last day of the medical clinic at Los Flores would change our lives and confirm our faith in God. As with any major life event, everyone will remember it differently. I will tell you what I remember from that day. Early in the day, Diane saw a baby for an infection and a fever, brought to the clinic by his grandmother. She gave him antibiotics and instructions on fever control. Later that day, the baby's mother came to my clinic station for herself. When I was done seeing her, she would not leave. I brought Abby over to help translate what she was saying. Her baby was sick, and she was trying to communicate that he needed help. The baby was not at the clinic, and I was confused as to what the mother was trying to tell me was wrong. I told Abby to apologize to the mother but tell her I could not help her without seeing the baby. Diane came over and told me she had seen and treated the baby earlier and we thought the problem was resolved.

Less than an hour later, while we were all piling in the back of the truck for our nightly river bath, Diane and Amy needed a quick bathroom break. I remember looking out across the field and seeing a group of people walking rapidly toward us. At the head of the group was the Grandmother Diane had seen earlier carrying a bundle. The woman was at the truck talking in rapid Spanish with Oscar Vasquez before I glanced over and saw the baby.

One look at that child and I swear I vaulted out of the truck in less than a second. The child was grey, his eyes were unblinking, breathing labored, and he had no tone to his muscles. I think we all realized at the same time the major crisis we were dealing with. I asked the Grandmother for the baby, yelled for Tylenol and my stethoscope and ran across the field to the medical clinic door. I knew in my heart that this baby was fading fast and there was little we were going to be able to do with limited medical equipment in a rural Honduran village.

When the clinic door was unlocked, we placed the baby on a table and began to assist him with the fight of his life. Diane began to check a rectal temperature and cut away the boy's clothing. The dial read 107.6 before she removed it, and it may have still been climbing. Listening to the child's heart was difficult as it was beating so fast. It felt like a hummingbird against his chest. Liquid Tylenol was found, and we gave it the only way we could, rectally. I also had a bulb syringe and started pushing in rectal fluid. We covered the baby in wet cold towels which were changed every few seconds. This child was uncomfortably hot to the touch in his core, with icy cold arms and legs. He was breathing like a runner after a marathon and his eyes remained unblinking on his colorless face.

At this point Robyn, who was busy getting us boiling water, suggested submerging the baby in the buckets of water, which Oscar Serrano and I immediately did, while Diane and others scooped cool water over his head. The child had a shallow response, so I slowly gave him water with an infant dropper. Every few minutes, we removed the baby from the water and percussed his back to help him clear the secretions which were further impairing his already decreased breathing effort. After twenty minutes of this rhythm, his temperature was rechecked, and the thermometer read 106 degrees. There was still no response from the baby to noise or pain.

It was nothing short of divine intervention when someone found infant ibuprofen, another medication used to break a fever. We had been in Las Flores for three days and not one of us had seen the bottle. Baby was given a large dose orally, since he could swallow. We continued to submerge him in water, changing buckets every few minutes. Marcel and Miguel always had a fresh bucket to change out, and Diane was ready to continue pouring cool water over the child's head.

The baby began grunting slightly with percussion and fighting with his legs when we placed him in the cool water buckets. Diane remembered that she had brought an inhaler we could use to open his lungs with (she had not used an inhaler in fifteen years) and we fashioned a seal with a Styrofoam cup to give the medication to the baby. After a few puffs, the baby's lungs dramatically improved. Another temperature showed a drop to 104 degrees.

When the Tylenol and Ibuprofen began to take effect, we knew. The baby began turning his head, showing discomfort, and blinking. He was still taking small amounts of oral water. His heart rate slowed and breathing became less shallow and more regular. I remember him turning his face toward his mother who was a short distance away and steadily chanting to God to save her baby. Another few minutes and the baby began to chill. His temperature was 100.6 and the fever had broken. We took him out of the water and called his mother over to see him.

When the baby, Juan Martinez, whimpered and cried minutes later, there was not a dry eye in the room. I swear it was the sweetest sound I had ever heard. I honestly had little hope for this child returning to us and think that the sheer will, faith, and determination of this group completely changed the outcome of this little fighter's life. We gave the mother several medications and strict instructions for controlling the fever. The local nurse was with the mother during the teaching as well. I am sure we will have little chance to know how Juan Martinez recovers, but I know that he will remain in the hearts of every person in that room on that fateful Wednesday afternoon.

What an incredible experience to get to witness God intervene and save that little baby's life! It was an experience none of us will ever forget. The next night, Honduras began to shake, literally! I did not go with the team to the mountains, as I had stayed behind to care for our girls. It was in the middle of the night when my daughter ran into the room saying, "Mommy, what happening?" I could hear as things began to rattle around in our home. Then, the shaking became intensely violent! I thought for one second that surely the roof would crash down on us at any moment. It was the most violent act of nature that I had ever experienced. I could hear outside, as the water from the swimming pool was now shaking out of the pool and onto the back porch. I could hear as the stone wall out back was being split down the middle. The shaking stopped, the power was out, and we were in total darkness. What had happened?

Just a few months before the earthquake, when we were building our house, Oscar took me to see the foundation of the first floor, explaining to me how well it was being made. I asked about how earthquake proof it was. It was at that time that Marcel, who was with us told me, "Amy there are no earthquakes in Honduras!" I told him that the country sits right on a major fault. He told me that not even his mother or grandmother or their parents before them had ever heard of an earthquake in Honduras.

We had no phone, no radio, no power and no way to get out into the outside world. One of our church members, knowing that I was alone with the girls, drove to our home to see if we were okay. He had also not heard what had happed or how bad it was. I knew obviously that it was an earthquake, but where? The most devastating natural disaster to ever hit Central America was the Guatemalan earthquake of 1974. The epicenter of that earthquake was very near the Honduran/Guatemalan border, right where Oscar and the team were in Las Flores. I had no way to contact them and feared terribly for their safety.

Finally, around 3:00 am the phone service came back on, but there was no signal to Las Flores. Around 4:30 am our phone rang. It was some friends in Tennessee telling us that they were just waking up and turning on the news to find that Honduras had just been rocked by a 7.3 magnitude earthquake. I asked them if the news was reporting where the epicenter was, and they said that it was actually out at sea near Roatán Island. This is the opposite direction from Las Flores, so I felt a sense of relief, but knew that we were not out of the woods; I still wanted and needed to hear from my husband and the rest of the team.

Oscar, up in Las Flores, was shaken awake by the violent earthquake and began to worry about us. They did have some battery powered radios that they could hear the news with. Though the earthquake was out at sea, the hardest hit area was Puerto Cortes, and of course that was what the news reported. Oscar gathered the team and was frantic to get down the mountain to call and see if we were okay. By 7:30 that morning, he was finally able to call, and we were both overjoyed that everyone was okay.

The earthquake, by the mighty grace of God, though mighty and strong, was virtually a dud in its impact. The port had suffered only minimal damage. Some bridges were down, and streets were cracked, but other than that, Honduras had dodged a major bullet. Just as soon as the phone came back, I called out to the Village and all our kids were safe and sound. Zulema, one of our main house mothers, told me that several of the kids didn't even wake up! We thought we had dodged a bullet at the Village as well but would soon discover we had not gotten off that easy.

This was also the time when the financial recession in the United States began to take its toll on H2H. As the situation in the US deteriorated, sponsors began to call one by one to let us know that they were no longer able to give. In total that year we lost nearly 70 sponsors. In addition, the political situation escalated. Mel Zelaya increased minimum wage a staggering 300% and the increase happened basically overnight. Just as our donor income was cut in half, our monthly expenses to pay our Honduran staff went up $5,000 per month or $60,000 per year, as we are required to pay double wages twice a year!

These were the years of famine. In the midst of this, another tragedy struck us. When we first came to Honduras, the property where the Village is located was donated by Salomon Lopez, the owner of the General Electric (GE) franchise in Honduras. When we went to have the Honduran power company put a meter at the Village, they told us that the property was owned by Salomon and they did not charge him for power, because they traded him power for equipment. So basically, they refused to put a meter at the property. We continued to ask for the meter, once the property was in our name, but then were told that they did not charge nonprofits. However, no one would give us a document to support this claim.

Now the summer of 2009 rolled around and we got a surprise visit from the power company. The man asked us why we were not paying for our power, and we gave him the explanation. He told us, he really didn't know who was in charge when we were told these things, but as far as he could tell, we owed for all our back-power use since 2000. In addition, we would need to pay a monthly power bill of $3,000 to $4,000 US Dollars per month. This was going to wipe our ministry out. We simply did NOT have this money. On top of all of that, Oscar was given a court order to go before the judge to be ordered to pay $250,000 USD, or the Village would be confiscated by the government!

Wait, there is more. If you think this year could not get any worse, you are wrong. On June 28th, after going against a Supreme Court order, Honduran President Mel Zelaya was arrested and ordered out of the country in a military coup. The vice president took over interim presidency of the country. The US government ruled the coup "illegal" and began to put heavy sanctions on Honduras, as did many other nations around the world. Now this already poor country was going to be punished even more! The country was torn apart between those supporting Zelaya's "primero los pobres" (the poor come first) government and the opposing leftist ideology that came with it. The country had been critically wounded.

Then on September 21st, Zelaya and his wife appeared back in Honduras after being banished in the coup, this time hiding out in the Brazilian Embassy. Martial law was put in place and the whole country was under a strict curfew. Those who supported Zelaya paid no attention and took to the streets and looted and protested. The US government sent out an urgent message that all non-essential government workers leave immediately. The Peace Corps pulled out and many other NGO's (Non-Governmental Organizations) pulled up stakes in Honduras.

We met together as a board and decided that we needed to call all our teams which were scheduled for the rest of the year, about fifteen groups, to let them know the situation. All but one decided not to come. Our lone group that year was led by a very brave woman from Castle Rock, Washington. She had been on many teams before, and this was to be a VBS team. Mary called her and explained the situation and asked her to pray about whether to come, because her team was scheduled for the most potentially dangerous time in November, right when the elections were to happen. This was expected to be a very volatile time. She told Mary that she did not need to pray about it. She said God told her that she was to come to Honduras and that it was in God's hands. She was not going to let the kids down. That woman's name was Carol Rutledge, a very brave missionary. Carol was killed in a car accident in Castle Rock, WA in 2013, but her courage still lives on in H2H.

We weren't sure what we should do about the power bill situation but decided to call Salomon Lopez to see if he could be of any help. We told him over the phone the gist of what was going on, and he suggested that we invite the Mayor of Omoa to be part of the conversation. We met with the two men in the middle of a corn field in the middle of nowhere. It was Salomon's agriculture project that he was very proud of. We explained the situation to the mayor, who immediately called the manager of the power company. With the phone in speaker phone mode, the manager said that we did NOT have to pay the back-owed funds, and that we did not have to pay monthly. This erased the court order for a time, but as we would learn over the years, this was not the end of the problem.

VBS team

Christmas with the Eliots in front of the Heart to Heart church 2009

Christmas shopping 2009

The entire Heart to Heart Children's Village - 2009

14
A Year of Amazing Firsts

"Let us therefore come boldly unto the throne of grace, that we may obtain mercy, and find grace to help in time of need." (Hebrews 4:16)

As I ended the chapter on the events of 2009, I prepared you for the onset of a few bad years that were to follow. It is interesting; I know they happened, because I lived them. It was in the summer of 2010 that Oscar and I put our house up for sale in order to keep food on the table for our eighty-five children. Fortunately, it never sold. As I reviewed old emails and ministry publications from that year, what I found, astoundingly enough, was tremendous growth and a year of many firsts and blessings! Even though funds grew tighter and tighter, God expanded the ministry. What is so cool about this is that the growth and advancements were nothing less than a miracle! This year, we were looking for anything and everything that we weren't using that we could sell to keep the ministry alive. What I am about to tell you is inexplicable. But God!

Mary sent an email out to a few close friends of the ministry explaining the situation, and it began as follows; "For the last three years we have been $5,000 a month short." Upon reading this, my immediate thought was, well how on earth have we kept going? By the grace of God! It reminds me of the Footprints poem; in the tough times, He carried us. So, as you read the details of this year, know this: It was filled with sleepless nights, economic famine, continued political problems and growing security problems. Welcome to 2010 in Worldwide Heart to Heart Ministries.

2010 was a great year of firsts. What I mean by that is, programs were initiated that continue strong today. The big first that year was the establishment of the Summer English Immersion Program (SEIP), a long name for "kids go to the US to visit their sponsors". We had talked for years about the possibility of some of the kids coming to the states to have that once-in-a-lifetime experience. We had already been through the process when we sent David for his club foot surgery, so we knew what was involved. We felt that many of our kids were sponsored by people who had a very long, close history with the ministry, and we felt we could potentially have the kids visit them in the US.

Three families were the first to sponsor the kids they supported to come to the states. The first kids to go were Marlon, our child who came to us from the garbage dump at Pizza Hut, Ilcy, Nelson and Adonis our first girl and her brothers, and Luis and Oscar two other brothers.

The idea was that the kids would spend the entire summer with their host families in the US. It was a much bigger project than I had imagined it would be. We had to get permissions from just about every government agency in the country, and that has only become more difficult to do over the years. It took time, but the judge finally allowed the kids to travel.

We worked tirelessly to get all their paperwork ready for the embassy appointment, which was an amazing process all on its own. The final papers were finished in San Pedro Sula at 9:00 pm the night before their 7:00 am appointment in Tegucigalpa, six hours away. We finished the paperwork, drove all night to Tegucigalpa, slept for three hours and went to our appointment. At the appointment, the immigration officer told us that the visa would be approved contingent on us providing a few more documents. That meant we had to turn around, drive back to San Pedro Sula and return to Tegucigalpa again the next day to submit the extra documents. It was a small price to pay for an unforgettable life changing summer for the kids.

Today, each summer, up to ten kids get to spend six to seven weeks with their sponsors in the US. Sponsors must be board members or long-time friends of the ministry. The year before we started the program, a friend who runs a children's home near us sent one of her girls to the US, as she was going to an established summer camp program. We figured if we were going to send the kids to the states, it should look official and have a fancy name and be sold as a "camp", so we created the name "Summer English Immersion Program" (SEIP).

We established rules for the program. An "English Only" zone should be created for the kids at their sponsor's home. The kids would live like any other sibling in the home, with chores and privileges. The kids could not "work", be used as a servant, or have a paying job. One hour of English instruction should be given each day. The children should see as much of the US as possible and be exposed to the food, culture, language and history of the country. The objective was in no way to try to "Americanize" the kids, but to give them a more rounded understanding of another culture and a more worldwide perspective. It was also to reawaken something that had died in many of our kids, the audacity to dream again.

When they came to the US, they saw opportunities and understood that many come with privilege, but some come with persistence. They saw the world as bigger than they had imagined it to be and filled with many ways of living, eating and thinking. This opened their eyes and their minds to the world as a mission field. Though many wished to serve God in Honduras, they also understand that many of the resources to do so can be found in its wealthier neighbor to the north, the US.

An exciting update is on one of the kids who was part of the first SEIP group in 2010. In the summer of 2015, Luis traveled back to the US and started college in Oregon, while living with his sponsor family. Luis is the "Billy Graham" of Puerto Cortes. He lives for bringing Christ to his country, but Luis has a plan. He was born and raised in the slums of San Pedro Sula. His parents went to work and left Luis and his smaller brother home alone with nothing to eat. Luis spent much of his time in the streets begging for food and ended up being put in the public orphanage a few times. Luis had a severe case of pica, a condition that forces a child to eat dirt or whatever they can to survive. Due to that fact, pica victims usually end up with dangerous and sometimes fatal parasitic infections. He told us that he wants to study medicine and meet lots of people. He wants to ask them if they want to go with him to Honduras and help lots more people who are poor and need Jesus. He wants to come back and start a ministry in Honduras, reaching out as a medical missionary.

The first summer SEIP was a great success! None of the children cried to stay with their host families. When the time was up, they were excited to see the other kids at the Village again. We have now run successful Summer English Immersion Programs each summer since. In this program, the sponsor family pays all the fees for the child's visit to the states, and no financial burden is placed on the ministry.

That year we also had our first Quinceañera. For those of you who are not familiar with the tradition, it is a custom celebrated throughout Latin America and could be compared to a glorified sweet sixteen coming out party. The tradition goes all the way back to old Spain, when at fifteen years of age, a girl was considered eligible for marriage. Her parents would dress her in the family's finest clothing and make her as beautiful as possible. They would take her down to the town square and stand her on the podium, letting all the eligible bachelors know that she was available. We have no intention of marrying off any of our fifteen-year-old daughters, but it is our custom in Honduras to throw a special party for the girls' fifteenth birthdays.

That year, one of our older girls turned fifteen and her sponsors, familiar with the tradition, asked if we would be doing a Quinceañera for her. We had never thought about it, but with the financial situation as it was, we just couldn't. The sponsors told us they would not be willing to divert the funds that they pledged to the general needs of the ministry to this event, but they really wanted their sponsored girl to have the Quinceañera. We realized that four other girls were also turning fifteen.

So that July, with the extra gift from that sponsor, we had the most beautiful, magnificent celebration of their lives. As each of the five came forward in her ball gown, I thought back to the day and the way they had arrived at the Village. One, as a young girl, had witnessed her father murdered by a rival gang, one was raped and abused by her stepfather, another was left abandoned by her father at a fast food restaurant, and two others were victims of malnourishment, poverty and abuse. As they marched forward that day in their beautiful dresses, they were so far removed from that prior reality. After years of rejection, hunger and abuse, here was a day to celebrate their lives. And this is what this ministry is really all about, the lost being found, the blind receiving sight and the dead coming back to life!

Since then, we have had four Quinceañera celebrations with our fifteen-year-old girls at the Village. We normally celebrate in November. Each year the party is privately sponsored by supporters who wish to designate the funds specifically for this event.

That year we met Dave and Paula Fester. They came down with their church, which also runs the ministry, Medical Relief International. They were with our dental team which visited our kids each year. The Festers were not dentists but wanted to run a small soccer program with the kids as they were getting their teeth cleaned. That was the first of what eventually became a major soccer program each summer.

The Festers became part of the H2H board of directors and returned the next year with a major summer camp program at the Village. It consisted of several days of intense soccer training. Then on the last two days, kids from the community were invited to join in. All the kids were divided according to age and the teams were put into brackets, until the last team standing won the grand prize. The kids were all given lunch, and then sat down to receive the message of salvation. Over the years many children have received Jesus through the annual soccer program.

Also, since Dave had been a former employee of Microsoft, he was able to get H2H into an amazing program within the company that allowed us to start receiving computers donated from

Microsoft. Over the next several years, we received many state-of-the-art computers. Today our kids in Honduras can stand side by side with kids of other developed nations in the area of technology, and our administrative staff is fully outfitted with the technology we need to operate this organization. This was an amazing blessing!

Finally, that year was also the beginning of our annual fundraising banquet in Portland Oregon. Kim Stephens and her husband Rick joined the ministry in 2009. Rick who is an accountant, took on the accounting for the ministry. Kim proposed that we do a banquet each year in our home city, and she has been the chairperson of that banquet each year since. Over the years, especially in the years of famine, we have depended heavily on the funds raised at this banquet.

Then there were the other amazing things that began that year. This was the year that the H2H clinic was started. Years before, we had been given a clinic worth of medical and dental supplies. Since Rick Stephens, one of our board members, worked at a dental equipment supply company, he was able to secure the donation of a dental chair with all its attachments and trays. Also, a clinic in a nearby town was closing and passed all their dental tools and equipment to us. We had a shell of a building on our church property that we wanted to make into a medical clinic which would serve our kids first and then the community. The nurse who had been running the clinic at the Village could no longer run it, and it had been closed a few years earlier. Because we were hurting so badly financially, we had no idea where we would come up with the funds to establish and build this clinic.

We received a phone call from a friend who believed that we could make an application to city hall, and they would help with the project. We made the application, and to our surprise, they agreed to supply the funds for the roof, $3,000. Over the next several months, Mercy Ships continued to send teams that further completed the construction. Today the clinic serves our children with medical and dental care. It also serves the community with low cost or free medical care for the very poor. The atmosphere of the clinic is one where the Spirit of God moves. Christian music and videos are shown in the lobby. Each patient is given a tract with the plan of salvation on it and is prayed for.

This year was also the beginning of an amazing relationship with Pastor Tom and Paula Graves. We had met them years before but had no idea what would become of the relationship. Back in 2007, a mutual friend invited us to do a presentation about the ministry to his church in Aberdeen, Washington. It was a small Lutheran church that was dying or almost dead. When we presented about our ministry, no one in the church appeared to care. No one was even paying attention. We noticed that the pastor, a man with a great heart, loved his church and was doing all that he could to breathe some life into it. He preached a great message about going out of our comfort zone to reach those around us, but the message fell on deaf ears.

After the service, Mary and I were in the foyer waiting for the congregation to come pick up information about helping H2H. No one did. I said to Mary, "Why are we here? She replied, "I know. I feel so sorry for Pastor Tom, because he is really ministering to these folks." When the pastor came out to the foyer, Mary felt God wanted her to pray for Pastor Tom. She held his hand and told him that she could see that he was suffering greatly regarding his position in the church, and she thought that God would use him one day to lead Evangelical crusades in Honduras.

This prayer was so random, and so out in left field, it would have been considered insanity if it had not come completely true! A few years went by and we had lost contact with Pastor Tom. One day, December 21st, 2009, Mary received a phone call from Wisconsin Rapids, Wisconsin. The woman said her name was Wendy Schlaefer, and she was the secretary of a church called St. Luke's Lutheran Church in Wisconsin Rapids. She was calling Mary because her church had just hired a new pastor who wanted to begin an orphan ministry. He told her to call Mary Frenter. The pastor's name was Tom Graves.

A few years after we presented at their church in Aberdeen, Washington, Pastor Tom and his family moved back to their ancestral home of Wisconsin and began to Pastor St Luke's

Lutheran Church. Now our lives were crossing paths once again. The truth was we never really understood how important our visit to Pastor Tom was for him. He said it was the first time anyone had ever spoken over him a word of knowledge and was the breath of fresh air that got him through the next few years.

In April of 2010, Lyle and Mary headed to Wisconsin by invitation from Pastor Tom to tell his church about H2H. After three services and a lovely dinner at Tom and Paula's home, he told Mary that when she prayed for him three years earlier, it was the first time he heard from the Holy Spirit, but it had not been the last.

In July of 2010, Pastor Tom and Paula, and a few members of St Luke's made their first trip to H2H ministries in Honduras. While here, Tom asked me what our kids needed. My response was spiritual healing. He said he knew just the person to help with this. His name was Bruce Van Natta, and by January 2011, Bruce was on his way to Honduras to do just that, pray spiritual healing over our children and many other people as well. This would be the first of several crusades which saw thousands saved and healed through the ministry of Pastor Tom and Bruce over the next four years.

If any of you can remember the world headlines from 2010, perhaps you will remember the biggest story of the year, the massive earthquake in Haiti. I remember driving back with Oscar from running errands in San Pedro Sula. We heard announced over the radio that there was a Tsunami warning in Puerto Cortes, but we could not find out why.

Once we arrived home and turned on the news, we were shocked to see what had happened. We watched the reports throughout the night as the news became more and more grim. Many tragedies happen around the world, and we are called to pray for God to intervene. However, in this situation, we could not find peace by just praying. As time went on, the need to go help became stronger and stronger. I remember talking with Mary and asking her if she was seeing what was going on there. When I said that, she responded with a heavy heart, that it had been weighing on her heart as well. We both knew that God was asking us as a ministry to go.

Our ministry was hurting financially, badly hurting, but God never wanted us to be comfortable or to feel in control. Often, he calls us out on the water and asks us to trust, in complete faith, without understanding why. We simply put it out there. Should we go as a ministry to Haiti? Within a few weeks, two of our board members signed up for the trip, Wil Meckle and Sondi Ross. Then it occurred to us that perhaps now was the time to teach the kids we were raising how to take what they were given and use it to love and care for others. Marvin and Josué were now 21 and 20 years old. They had been raised and educated at the Village, and they were now ready to serve. With Oscar leading the way, the five-person team was assembled and ready to go.

We had many challenges facing us. First, we did not know anyone in Haiti. Where would they go? The airport in Haiti was closed, so we did not even know how they would fly in. But most of all, what would they do? They did not want to go as sightseers; they wanted to go to bring hope and healing, in some way, to this hurting nation. We connected with another organization which was going down to help rebuild destroyed children's homes and felt that this was the direction that God was leading us to go. Our five missionaries joined that team. The plan was that they would go and work with this ministry for one week, and then see what God would have them do thereafter.

The team had to land in San Jose, Dominican Republic as the airport in Port-au-Prince, Haiti, was not open. This meant enduring an eight-hour drive to the small village that was about two hours outside of Port-au-Prince where they would be working. Since the building had been destroyed, they had to sleep outside in tents. Before they left, I packed our boys lots of snacks that I thought they could share with the hungry kids on the streets. However, they would soon find out that it was going to be their only sustenance for the next two weeks.

When they arrived at the children's home, they found a shocking situation. Haiti was already the poorest nation in the western Hemisphere, and that was before the earthquake. Now the country was in absolute crisis. Oscar said that he had cash and two credit cards and still could not get anything to eat. He told us that out on the road, only small, goldfish-sized fish were for sale to eat. The rivers were not even navigable, as they were filled with trash, sewage and even human bodies; and this was where those fish came from! The children's home was a horrible place run by hardened people. Each night Oscar said the children cried through the night due to extreme hunger. The team went to work to help build a wall for storing the trash. While they were there, they also went to buy underwear for the kids.

After the week was over, the team met a man who agreed to come and pick them up and take them to Port-au-Prince. The man's name was Sammy Love, and he turned out to be a wonderful Christian man. He took the team to his home, and his family allowed them to stay with them and fed and cared for them. Sammy also took the team around to see the true need in Haiti. On one of those trips, he took the team to see one of the many tent cities in Port-au-Prince. In these cities, thousands of destitute families were surviving only by the grace of God.

Oscar recounted his experience on one visit to the tent city. He said that they arrived and walked through aisles and aisles of hopelessness. Each family was on the verge of death, and many had not eaten in days. Each family was slowly watching their children perish. As Oscar began to speak with them, he could see two things: number one; the people were in a very precarious situation, and number two; it was not a situation that they were unfamiliar with. They were in danger and they knew it, but this was not their first rodeo. If there were any people in the world who could survive this, it would be the Haitians.

The team gathered with the people they had met and prayed. Oscar said the worst part of the whole thing was that they were there just staring at the people and feeling sorry for them. As they gathered together, they prayed that by faith God would send them the food they needed by the next day. When they left, Oscar asked Sammy not to take them to any more tent cities; he could not go anymore and offer them nothing. Oscar and the team were hoping for a miracle. Many of these people had been raised in voodoo and knew nothing about God, but he knew that they were trusting in God to provide.

The next day was Sunday, and the team planned to go to church. They were going to go to Sammy's church, but realized that due to the culture of the church, Sondi, as a woman, would not be allowed to go unless she wore a skirt or dress. Since they had basically been backpacking, Sondi had not thought to bring a dress, so Sammy had another idea. There was another church on the other side of town called the International Church. Sammy said that he understood that many missionaries went there and that the services were in English. The team joined that church for Sunday service and just as Sammy said, many "white" missionaries were present. The team sat in the back, and Oscar said that a woman who looked vaguely familiar at the front of the church kept looking back at him. He knew he knew her but could not remember from where. By the end of the service the woman ran back to him and said, "Oscar Serrano, is that you"? Now he remembered. It was Kathy Cadden, of Operation Ukraine.

Two year ago, we had become acquainted with Kathy, who lived in Alabama and worked for an organization that sends containers to many different places in the world. Operation Ukraine sent a container to Honduras, and we had a chance to meet with Kathy in 2008 in Dallas, Texas. Kathy was now in Haiti trying to do all that she could to meet the great need in this country.

She told Oscar to follow her. She wanted to show him what she had been doing. She brought him to a warehouse behind the church that was packed with buckets filled with food. She told him that she had just received two containers full of food and was waiting to receive forty more. She said that they wanted to get food to as many people as they could. Oscar told her, "You won't believe what happened to us yesterday." He explained to Kathy all that had happened at the tent city and told her that he had believed a miracle would happen to provide for those people. Kathy asked him to tell her the exact location of this tent city. She said, "Don't worry, Oscar. Tomorrow we will go and feed those people." What a glorious answer to prayer!

That year something amazing happened with one of our kids that truly showed them that God was alive and doing amazing things in their lives. Marlon had always suffered with a horrible case of gastritis. He would often come to our home on the weekends, and I had to be extremely careful with whatever I cooked when he came for dinner. His diet basically consisted of plain rice, corn tortillas, and bland vegetables.

One night at our church a message about supernatural healing was given, and the congregation was told to trust God for the healing that they needed. Many came forward and were prayed for, and Marlon was one of them. He knew that he needed healing and thought to himself, "It can't hurt. I should just go forward." Without "great faith" Marlon went forward and trusted God to heal him. He said he did not feel anything happen to him, but still trusted that perhaps God had done something. So that night, just to see, he made something to eat that would normally cause him a great deal of pain, spicy food. He said, "I don't know what happened. I cooked. I ate. I went to sleep. No pain; no worries!" The next morning, he was shocked and said, "I just really needed to know for sure." He made himself a spicy, fried concoction that he never would have tolerated before. He ate it, and he enjoyed it. He has never had a problem with food or gastritis again!

That year we were also very disappointed with an event that happed at the Village. Up to this point we had never had any challenges with robbery in any form. Currently, the girls were taking beauty classes in Tegucigalpita. Two years earlier we had received the donation of a totally outfitted beauty salon school, which included the furniture, the equipment and the products. We had only two nighttime guards at the Village. One night, around 2:00 am, the girls' house head mommy called both on-duty guards. Out in the street in front of the girls' house, several men with sheets over their heads were walking around making strange noises. Because this was a suspicious event, both guards went to the girls' house to be a visible presence there. What we didn't know was that it was a diversion so the heist could take place at the other end of our property.

Down on the other end of the property was the boys' house, and the Tech School, where the beauty salon was. With both guards down at the girls' house attending to the bogus spectacle on the street, other members of this motley crew were breaking into our salon and taking all of our dryers, straighteners, curlers, rollers, and hundreds of dollars' worth of product.

The next morning, as the girls made their way to classes, they found the outside door broken in and the salon a mess with all of their things gone. We were so heart broken. It is bad to steal from anyone but stealing from orphans is as low as you can get.

We let all our sponsors know through our monthly newsletter what had happened and that for now the classes had been canceled. This was a huge disappointment. Our girls had worked so hard and were only months from getting their degrees as beauticians. At that point I could not even begin to offer the girls any hope of getting back to their lessons any time soon. But true to the nature of our wonderful sponsors, items began to pour back in. From many different sources, from beauty salons and from those not even associated with salons, funds and equipment began to come in to replace the things that had been lost. We were down, but not for long! Within a few months the classes resumed with the supplies and equipment all replaced. The teacher even told me that many of the replacement supplies were better than what we had before.

To cap off the year, we had an amazing event. The wonderful young man who had come to us as a gang member, running away from the evil way of life that was chasing him, married his American missionary wife. Marvin and Karen were married in December of that year. Oscar and I, Mary and Lyle, and many other members of our board and H2H supporters descended on Tennessee for a week-long celebration, culminating in the wedding which Oscar and I officiated. During the week, we had a board meeting in the conference room of the hotel where we were staying. Since our Village children had only attended 76 of the required 200 days of classes that year because of teacher strikes, we decided we needed to begin plans to build our own school and ensure our children got an education.

The year 2010, despite the financial turmoil, was an amazing year. Since we had no money, no resources, and no ability to do all of this ourselves, God was all the more glorified in our circumstances!

Luis Sagastumes, Oscar Sagastumes, Adonis Barias, Nelson Barias and David Bardal in the United States

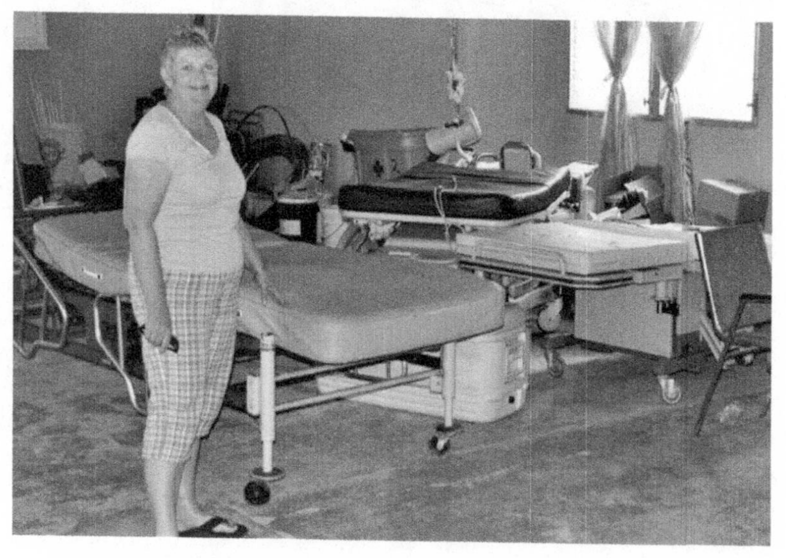

Jane Meckle with the new beds for the H2H clinic

First Quinceañera - 2010

2012

2013

2015

2018

2019

Rick Stephens helping out

Preparations & Gifts

1st Annual Soccer Camp & Tournament run by Dave & Paula Fester - 2010

2nd Annual Soccer Camp & Tournament - 2011

3rd Annual Soccer Camp & Tournament - 2012

4th Annual Soccer Camp & Tournament - 2013

Finishing building the H2H clinic

The kids from the Children's Village and Vacation Bible School team

Destruction after the earthquake in Haiti - 2010

Tent camps in Haiti

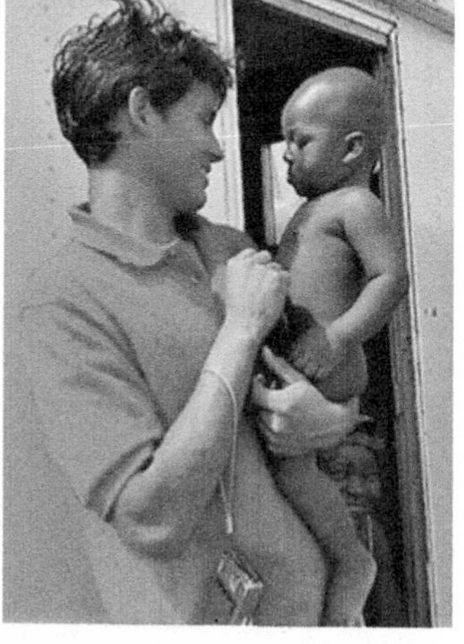

Visiting an orphanage in Haiti, Josué Hercules holding one of the kids

Group photo with the people and the older boys Marvin Ramos and Josué Hercules. Sondi Ross, Will Meckle. Oscar and other friends who helped

15

Miracles Abound

"Behold, I will do a new thing; now it shall spring forth; shall ye not know it? I will even make a way in the wilderness, and rivers in the desert." (*Isaiah 43:19*)

Just as 2010 was a remarkable year with many ups and downs, 2011 had victories and challenges of its own. This was the year that we met together as a board in the United States to see what direction we should go from here on out. Was God calling us to something new, perhaps a different direction? That summer we had a time of prayer and fasting to see what the Lord would tell us, and each board member was given the same word; that we were to continue in the direction that we were already going, and do what we were already doing, but strive for excellence. We could see many areas that were not excellent. The areas we sought to improve on the home front were education, health care, nutrition, Village staffing and finances.

By 2011, the public-school system of Honduras, where our kids were attending classes, had collapsed. Fighting within the department of education had caused the whole system to implode. The typical school year would be as follows; in February, as the school year runs from February to November, our kids' excitement would build as the new school year was upon us. We would purchase their new uniforms and school supplies, and then the first exciting day of school was upon us. When the kids returned home, the stories were grand, all about their new teachers and new classmates. Orientation day was always wonderful. All of the parents would go to the assembly and hear from the school director all the plans, hopes and dreams that were in store for the year. Each parent went away hopeful that it would not be like the year before, but no such luck.

If the first day of school was February 10th, then right on cue, sometime around 10:00 am on February 25th, we would see them coming around the corner, the first set of our kids, then a large trail behind them of not only our kids, but all the children of the community. They were sent home, no more classes, it was a teachers' strike. Classes would not resume until sometime perhaps in May. Go to school again, and then again in August Boom! no classes again until October. This was the story year after year. In 2010, our children had only gone to school 76 days out of the mandatory 200 required by law per school year. And instead of trying to catch the kids up to speed on what they had missed, they simply passed them ahead to the next grade. Our kids were dangerously behind where they needed to be in order to compete with other kids their age from around the world.

We decided that this was unacceptable. With all that these kids already had against them, lacking a good education would mean more of the same: stuck in a lifestyle with no way of breaking out of the cycle that brought them to us in the first place. It had become critical that we provide an alternative to the education our kids were getting. Home school not only does not exist in Honduras, it is illegal to educate your child at home, so the home school option was off the table. The only hope was to build our own school. The task seemed impossible to achieve, but God began to show us through many events that it was not that impossible after all.

Good Friends of H2H, Dan and Christine Moore from Virginia expressed that they wanted to help with the seed money to get a preschool and kindergarten class going at the Village. As many in education know, these are two of the most important grades in a child's academic life. The Moore's offered to put in the funds to build the classrooms and pay a year's worth of salary for a teacher. This was tremendous confirmation that we were going in the right direction. Not only that, but Ashley Kwasney, who had been involved with H2H since coming with our first mission team in 2000, told us that she and her husband, Gary, would be willing to come and help start and run the school. Ashley, a pastor from Montana, had worked in education in her home state for many years. Sarah Matoon, a young woman from Oregon, who had been on a team a few years prior and who was educated in music and art, volunteered to come and teach those subjects. As you read in the story of Marlon, she later married one of our first "sons".

School in Honduras is very interesting. The department of education is disorganized, and its requirements for a school are often not only unhelpful, they can be downright harmful to the education of a child. By Honduran law, we had to hire two Honduran teachers who did some teaching but served mostly to keep up the ridiculous handwritten ledger books that the department of education required.

That August, our Pre-school, Kindergarten and 1st grade at the Village became a reality. This was the start of something amazing, and we knew that it was only going to improve from there. We also knew that the Devil hated what we were doing. He hated the direction that we were going and what we were doing with excellence. He knew that it would begin to break chains and bring healing to many children. He did all within his power that year to stop what was happening.

In January of that year we met some wonderful new friends who would later become a huge part of our ministry. When Pastor Tom Graves of St. Luke's Lutheran Church in Wisconsin Rapids, Wisconsin came to visit our ministry in July of 2010, he told us about a friend that had an accident a few years earlier. His friend Bruce Van Natta had been a diesel mechanic in Wisconsin. God had been calling Bruce for years to go into full-time ministry, however Bruce resisted.

In 2006 on a routine service call, Bruce had a large logging truck fall on top of him which basically cut him in half. Bruce was dead and even had an out of body experience. A man named Bruce Carlson, whom Bruce Van Natta had met briefly a few years earlier, was woken up in the middle of the night and told to go and pray for Bruce. He flew from New York to Wisconsin that same night and prayed for him. What happened was a creative miracle in Bruce's body. He had lost almost all his small intestines in the accident and was now slowly starving to death. When Bruce Carlson prayed for him, nine feet of small intestines grew back.

After Bruce Van Natta had recovered, God called him to a healing ministry. When Pastor Tom was telling me the story of Bruce he said, "But not only does he have a physical healing ministry, he has an emotional healing ministry." He told me that as a child, Bruce was sexually abused, and had received an emotional healing from the Lord. Therefore, his ministry also focused on emotional healing. As the words were coming out of Pastor Tom's mouth, I knew that this Bruce Van Natta needed to come to Honduras to pray for our kids. I asked to talk to both of the Bruce's to see if they would agree to come and pray for our kids, who had also been abused in every way imaginable.

Soon after Pastor Tom returned to the states, he called to let us know that Bruce could come, but it would not be until May of the next year. When I heard that, I knew that was not right, I knew they needed to come sooner. I asked if they could pray and consider coming anytime sooner. After talking to them they agreed to come January of 2011.

In January of 2011 we had our first crusade with St Luke's Lutheran Church and Bruce Carlson and Bruce Van Natta. On the Honduras end, a tremendous amount of work went into preparing, not only in the natural realm, but also in the spiritual realm. It was decided that we would do the crusade at the local public school. For many months, our church daily prayed over the school. We fasted for several days and held prayer each morning at 5:00 am.

The crusade itself had lots of challenges. First, the acoustics in the old school gym were terrible. The music sounded like noise, and the voices were not even understandable. To make matters worse, the two days of the crusade turned into a torrentially down-pouring storm, one of the worst of the century! Since the building was metal roofed, that made the bad audio almost impossible to work with and hear over. All the same, many people were healed. The team also came to our Village and prayed over each child, and many received healing there.

We were also visited that year by the Church on the Mountain Woman's Conference. Several women from a small church at the foot of Mount Hood asked if they could come down and minister to the women of Honduras. All of the women were musicians and also brought the word of God. We had a beautiful candlelight worship service the first night with over 200 women in attendance. All day Saturday we heard teaching, worshipped and prayed for our women. Many women were saved, healed and set free of old roots of bitterness, sickness, and oppression. We could see that God was doing something amazing in Honduras.

This was also the year we got sweet, beautiful little Annie (not her real name) We got the call from the local police that a child had been rescued from a life of terrible abuse and wanted to know if we had room for her. Of course, we always have room for one more and told them to please bring her. The next day a sweet little two-year-old girl arrived at the Village, scared and shy. At first appearance, she did not look that bad off, she was plump and had a head full of hair, no signs of malnutrition. However, once her dirty, torn dress was removed, the reality was shocking. Her fragile two-year-old body was covered in bruises, burns and abrasions. Her stepfather had been physically abusive to her. Once the report was made to the police about her condition, they went to the house to arrest the parents and take the girl into their custody. Someone must have tipped the stepfather and mother off about the sting, because when the police arrived, they found only little Annie alone in the home. The father and mother have not been seen since.

Annie's physical injuries would soon heal, but it would take prayer, love and counseling to restore her broken heart and spirit. I am happy to report, she is now a happy six-year-old in first grade, who from all appearances, doesn't even remember the horrors of her infancy. "He will wipe every tear from their eyes". Revelation 21:4a.

As I said, the Devil was by no means going to let all of this go on without a fight. As I had mentioned in previous chapters, the political situation in Honduras had gone off the proverbial cliff. When the government collapsed, there was a vacuum of leadership and authority in the country, and true to its nature, every criminal syndicate known to man was ready and waiting to fill that void. By 2011, gang violence had risen in the country to numbers never seen before. Honduras had quickly become the most dangerous country in the world. That year San Pedro Sula, the industrial capitol of Honduras, had more civilian deaths due to violent crime per capita than anywhere else in the world. By 2013, Honduras would see more civilian deaths due to violent crime than Iraq in 2007 at the height of the Insurgency.

At this time entire communities were completely gang controlled. The police and other authorities were almost powerless to stop them for two reasons; number one, many cops were on the payroll of the bad guys, and number two, they were simply out gunned by the criminal elements.

On a sunny day in May, Oscar and I had just gone to the bank to withdraw over $3000 to replace the engine of one of our work trucks. Now you may ask, why on earth would we work in cash in such a dangerous society? Honduras in many ways was still a cash only society. Checks and credit cards had no value. We had been in Honduras for eight years and up until this time, had never had a bad experience. But as we were about to learn, Honduras had changed.

After leaving the bank, we went to meet the people who would be taking the money to the mechanic. We planned to meet them at the school, where we were picking up some of our teenage kids as they were dismissed. We drove up to the outside of the school, but our contact people had not yet arrived. The kids were already out of school and began to pile into the truck.

Oscar noticed two men walk by, looking very anxious. They walked about four yards past the truck and then returned. As Olga, one of our girls, was getting into the truck in the back cab, one of the men grabbed her by the hair and pulled her out. From the back door of the cab, he put a gun to Oscar's head and told him to hand him all the money. The other man came around the other side and began to pound on my door which locks automatically. Without hesitation, Oscar gave him the cash we had just pulled out of the bank.

He also ordered Oscar to give him the car keys, and both of our cell phones. As soon as they had these things, they simply walked away on foot. This was in broad daylight in front of over 200 students and school staff. Several of the school kids followed the men and said they had gotten into a tan four-door car around the corner about a block away, that had been waiting for them. One of the kids saw them throw the truck keys into the grass. The kid picked them up and brought them back to us.

After the incident, we went home and called the police. They never came. Oscar went to the bank the next day and reported what had happened and asked them to review the surveillance tapes to see who was in the bank at the same time he had been. He also went to the police station to report the incident. As he was giving his statement to the woman at the station, a man walked in who looked eerily similar to one of the men who had assaulted us the day before.

For those of you who know Oscar, you know he often speaks exactly what's on his mind. When the woman asked him what this man looked like, Oscar pointed and told her, "Exactly like that guy." At this point she seemed anxious but went on with the interview. She asked Oscar to describe the car that the kids reported seeing the men get into, and Oscar said it was a tan four-door. At this, the woman grew pale and stopped the interview telling him she had all the information she needed.

Once Oscar left the police station he understood why. Just outside the station was a tan four-door car. The officers had just arrived at the station during Oscar's interview in that car. To be completely fair and honest, to this day we do not know who the perpetrators were. Oscar did return to the bank the next day and was told that they could not show us the video, but did not think there was a problem, "The only people in the bank that day," they told him, "were a few cops."

Life went on, and we boiled it down to an isolated incident. After all, things like that happen in the US too. However, our worries were far from over. In November of that year, just one day before Thanksgiving, I headed out to the Village with all of the girls who live at our house to do letter writing with the kids. Around 10:00 am that morning Oscar called me and said, "You need to come home right away. Something really bad has happened. Our house was broken into and Melissa was tied up." Melissa was a friend who worked at our house as a housekeeper and helped us with all the cooking and laundry for all of the girls.

Around 8:00 am that morning, a white four door car pulled up at our house and four men got out. They tapped on the gate and told Melissa that they had a delivery for Oscar Serrano. They had a box in hand, and so she went down to retrieve the box. As soon as she got to the gate, they pointed a gun at her and demanded she let them in. Once inside, they took Melissa to the bathroom and tied her up. Then they began to go through the house, taking many of our things. In the office they took all the ministry computers, our TV, jewelry, cameras, and all the cash they could find. After about thirty minutes they left. Melissa told me, that she could hear two of them fighting about whether or not to kill her, as they were not wearing masks and she could identify them. Glory to God, they left Melissa shaken but otherwise unharmed and went their way. She was able to hop over to the neighbor's house and get help.

The next day was Thanksgiving and everyone was in a funk. I decided to try to turn the funk around and told the girls we would decorate the house for Christmas that day and make Thanksgiving dinner. Marvin was also flying in that night to visit for a few days, so we would go to the airport later to pick him up. I put on the Christmas music and the girls pulled out the tree and decorations. Smiles began to return and by the evening, as we all sat to eat together, we had decided to say, "Hallelujah anyway!"

We were sure that when our phones were stolen during the first assault back in May, they had gotten our personal information. We again called the police, and after several hours, they finally arrived at the house. They did some very unimpressive police work and left. We knew that we needed to do something to defend ourselves, so we purchased security cameras and had them installed around our house. Someone who had seen the car told us that they were pretty sure they knew the owner and where he lived. Oscar decided to borrow a friend's car and drive by the place where these people lived to get a picture of the car in question. When he showed it to Melissa, she said that it was the car that had come to the house, or at least it was one exactly like it.

Just a few days later, we had a few missionary friends from Guatemala staying at our house. Oscar and I had been invited to be "padrinos" at a graduation for a friend's daughter and the girls and the friends from Guatemala had gone to church. While we were at the graduation, we got a call from the girls saying we needed to go home right away, because the house had been broken into again. This time nothing was taken, something was left, a death threat! The only things they had taken were the cameras which had not yet been hooked up to the internet.

We called the police again, and this time they were at our home right away. Something about these police officers seemed sincere this time. There seemed to be something that we could trust. At this point it had become obvious, we had been targeted. As Oscar told the police officer about all that had happened since May, the officer told him, "Look, there are a few cops you can trust, and I think you should tell all of this to my boss." Reluctantly, but with no other options, Oscar agreed to trust him.

Within five minutes the chief was at our home, and Oscar took him to our office and told him everything. The chief told him that he was new in town and was going to start cleaning things up. He told Oscar that we had been lucky until now, and that several other families in our area had been targeted and had been murdered. This was not comforting! Since we had ten girls in our custody, the chief told us that he would provide twenty-four-hour police protection and from that night, we had an officer guarding our home 24/7.

The chief put one of his best men in charge of the investigation, a man the other officers knew as "Rambo". While watching the local news a few days later, we saw the chief of police talking on TV. He had made the very bold decision to fire almost the entire department.

Oscar, who was very untrusting of cops, could not decide if he was more afraid of the cop in our home, or the bad guys. He told me that this person could rape all our girls and get away with it because he had a badge. So, he decided to have one of our older boys guard the cop. Felipe, a young man who works for us, also came to live at our house to keep an eye on the police officer at night.

"Rambo" often called Oscar, but never with good news. Each time he found out a bit more about the situation, it got scarier for us. As it turned out, the roots of this got deeper and deeper and the characters involved were more and more sinister. It came to a point when Oscar almost had to tell him, please stop calling me.

I, on the other hand, went to work calling the American Embassy, which was a bad idea. They took my full report, and then urged us to leave Honduras. "What? We absolutely can't! What about the kids? We can't just abandon them," I told her. The woman on the other end seemed very concerned. "You really need to leave. We can't protect you, and once you receive a death threat, you must take it very seriously." This phone call rattled me and put a lot of fear in me. She said that all the other cases involving Americans they had worked with had not turned out well.

Still looking for some hope and some actual help, I called a friend who was ex FBI. This phone call was even worse! He told me that it would be stupid not to leave immediately. He told me that in all his years of law enforcement he had noticed a pattern. He said when a person has been targeted, the bad guys take and take until there is nothing left to take, and then they just kill you.

At this point I did begin to think, maybe we should leave. Maybe they are right. But something in my heart told me, no, this was just a deception! Encouragement did come from some very positive voices. Freddy Castro, one of Oscar's close friends and our church pastor, told us that he believed that the letter left in the house showed some fear. The letter mentioned something about "not messing with them". Since Oscar mentioned to the police that he had friends in the FBI and had contacted the embassy, Freddy thought they may be thinking we were too much of a risk and wanted *us* to "back off". As he was saying this, something in my spirit said, "Listen to that! That is completely true!"

Then a few days, later I received a call from Marvin in Tennessee. Normally when he calls and I answer the phone, we say our hellos and I pass the phone to Oscar. We talked for a few minutes and I told him that Oscar was not home, but Marvin said, "Actually, I called to talk to you." "Okay, what's up?" "Well, I just wanted to tell you a story about a man my wife knew."

He was from Tennessee and went to their church and sometime after college, felt a call to go to Africa. At that point there was a lot of civil war going on in the part of Africa that he wanted to go to, and everyone pleaded with him not to go. However, knowing that this was God's will for him, he went anyway. After a year of service in Africa, the man came home for a few weeks of sabbatical in the US and even brought an African man that he served with to visit his family. Two days before they were to return to Africa both men were killed in a car accident.

I totally understood the point of his message to me. That there was indeed a place more dangerous than Honduras at that time, and that was the place of being out of God's will. I could leave Honduras, return to the US, and get hit by a car, or I could stay in Honduras and perhaps die, but perhaps not. The thing is, we were in God's hands and needed to trust him.

Kim Stephens, one of our board members, had been talking with her daughter who went to a large church in California and knew a man who helped with security and was former military. He had started a new ministry to do exactly what we needed. He went into ministries such as ours to teach the members how to stay safe, even when their country or area was not safe. Within days, this man was on a plane and headed to Honduras. He spent four days with us and did intense training on how to move and operate in Honduras. Today we are much less trusting, much more cautious, and travel with security.

Even though we were unwilling to leave, we did take the advice of others and got our own daughters out of the country. Two American girls can bring in millions in ransom money. In December we were visited by our old friends Eric and Laura Smith.

They came during Christmas and brought lots of cheer to our home and made cookies and homemade fudge with the girls. The Smiths took our family to Roatán, and Oscar and I will both tell you; it was the first night that we had slept in weeks. When the Smiths flew out on December 28th, Sarah, Rachel, and I flew out with them. The girls were going to be living with Grandma Mary for the next several months until we could figure the situation out in Honduras. It is the most hurtful thing in this whole mess for me. Out of all that was stolen from us, the six months away from our girls was the most precious. It is six months of their childhood we will never get back.

Ashley and Gary Kwasney

Amy and Oscar with Dan Moore and Steve Robeson

16

Educating Our Kids

"For we wrestle not against flesh and blood, but against principalities, against powers, against the rulers of the darkness of this world, against spiritual wickedness in high places."
(Ephesians 6:12)

Just a few days after we left, Bruce Van Natta, Bruce Carlson, Pastor Tom and members of his church came to Honduras to do another crusade. This time it was going to be different. We called the crusade "Peace for our City". It wasn't just us; the entire country was getting sick of this situation. We had been praying for months that the men who had assaulted us would be at that crusade and get saved. Whether they were or not, we don't know. We gathered at the baseball stadium in Puerto Cortes, since many churches from our area were present. We cried out to God that night for healing, not only physical healing, but healing for our nation, and healing for our city. We invited the mayor and the chief of police and had them come forward and prayed for them. People at the crusade literally said they could see things breaking in the atmosphere!

Rambo continued to call Oscar and tell him that he was very close to taking down the group which was responsible for our troubles. One day, however, Rambo was at a local restaurant talking with the owner. This man was rumored to be involved in shady business dealings. Rambo was being guarded by other officers, when a cop car showed up at the restaurant and four men dressed as officers got out. They told the other officers guarding Rambo that they had urgent business that they needed to discuss with him. The guards let them in and once inside, they pulled out machine guns and killed Rambo, the restaurant owner, and one other man who was with them. The "cops" responsible were never caught.

But, just as quickly as our problems had begun, they now all stopped. In fact, many of the problems in Puerto Cortes stopped. Within a year, Puerto Cortes had won an award as the "safest city in Honduras". God had heard our prayers and had moved in a mighty way!

The biggest question for us this year was, how were we ever going to learn how to sleep through the night again? After so much time spent living with constant worry, it begins to take its toll on your body.

I remember a day that I was at my home alone. Marcel and Oscar had gone to the bank, as we now only go to the bank in groups. A red pickup truck arrived at the house. Two men got out and started banging on the gate, saying they were from the power company and to come open the gate. There was no marking on the vehicle that would suggest that they were from the power company, nor were they wearing any kind of a uniform. I could see the driver through a crack in my window, as he lifted his shirt and patted his stomach. "That's not the power company," was the thought that ran through my head. My heart felt like it stopped! I grabbed a knife and ran upstairs and hid on the outside of the balcony. I clutched my phone on the way up and sat outside frantically calling Oscar and Marcel but had no luck. The bank has a policy that you must either leave your cell phone outside or have it turned off while you are in the bank.

The men pounded the gate even more aggressively, shouting for someone to open it. Finally, Marcel called me back. I could only whisper "Marcel, there are some men at the house, please come soon." "What?" he shouted. "I can't hear you." "There are men at the house," I said a little louder. "Don't worry, Amy, we will be there as soon as we can!" he said. Soon after I hung up the phone, I saw the red truck driving away. Not sure if they might have left someone behind at the house, I stayed upstairs waiting and listening. Five minutes went by and then ten. I could hear nothing, nor did anyone else come to the house. After about fifteen minutes, I carefully made my way down the steps and into the living room and kitchen. All clear; I was alone. They had gone.

Five minutes later, Oscar and Marcel arrived at the house. What had taken them so long? I could have been dead by now. As it turns out, they had been down at the end of the street for the last ten minutes confronting the drunken electricians who the power company had hired to come to the house and cut off the power! The workers had been legitimate. I had a good laugh at myself, but I knew I had to get the peace of God in me once again. I certainly did not want to transmit worry and fear to our kids.

Oscar was no better than I was. He slept only a few hours each night, pacing the floors and looking out the window each time a small bump was heard. One night, as he frantically paced the halls, looking out each window for the boogey man to arrive, he clearly heard God speak to him, "Oscar go to bed, what are you doing?" "No Lord," he retorted, "I have to keep this family and all our girls safe, what if they come back?". The Lord responded, "The watchman guards in vain, if the Lord does not defend the city." Oscar realized that he was giving in to a spirit of fear, and decided he simply needed to go to bed and be done with the fear.

Little did we know that a huge blessing was in store for H2H and would be a game changer for the kids. As I mentioned in the last chapter, we had decided that we were going to become excellent, and first on the agenda was educating our kids. By August of 2011, we had a school functioning at the Village that served Pre-school through 2nd grade. This had been possible through some wonderful friends and their generous donations and service.

At the beginning of 2012, we were joined by Jordan Rinta, an associate pastor in Centralia, Washington. Jordan had a good job, wonderful family and friends, and all that he could have ever wanted, except for peace. Jordan had been to Honduras with his church on a mission trip to Tegucigalpa. During that trip, God began to show him that he wanted him to move out of his comfort zone into something else. One day, he was sharing this with his good friend, Gerardo Ramirez, a young man who Oscar and I had known since his youth. Gerardo had been to Honduras on many occasions and had always been very close to our ministry. Jordan shared with Gerardo that he was very dissatisfied with life in the states and felt that God was calling him to the mission field. Gerardo told him he should check out WWH2H, so in January Jordan came for two weeks and then returned in May long-term.

In November 2011, as we do every year, we had a yearly fundraising banquet. We had decided that we would focus on building a bigger home for the teen boys as the home that we currently had was only big enough to house about eight boys. As many of our teens were growing quickly, we were going to need a lot more room. We had a beautiful hand drawn sketch by Freddy of what the future building would look like, and I headed to Oregon to speak at our banquet. Our other speaker that night was Bruce Van Natta. We focused on getting more sponsors for the children and the funds needed for the Teen Boys' home, but in the end, God will do what he wants to do!

Two very good friends who helped us build the Baby House in 2008 and 2009 were at the banquet that night. They listened as Mary spoke briefly about our concerns for the education of our kids. After the banquet, Mary was in Honduras with our Christmas Prep team. She received an email from this couple. It said they had come to the banquet intending to give a donation that we could put in the bank and use for the college education of our kids in the future. After listening to Mary speak, they realized the kids were never going to make it to college, because they were not getting an elementary and high school education that would prepare them for that. They said they were sending a donation of $100,000 that they wanted designated toward building our own school for the education of our kids. We were shocked, amazed and praised God! The truth is Marvin, Josué and Marlon had all tried college, but with the inadequate education they had received, they simply could not make it. It was those boys who told us to find a better way to educate all the kids.

This was a tremendous experience! We were still running

$5,000 a month short of our monthly needs just to maintain what we were already doing. In addition, the political, security and economic situation in Honduras became worse with each passing day. Our board became very fractured over this situation. Some of us believed that this was what the Lord had provided, and it was designated for this cause. Others believed that though we could not use the funds for anything other than education, it was not the time to start a major capital endeavor such as building a full-scale school!

We debated putting the school out at the Village, but we had two challenges with the scenario: first, we did not want our kids to have NO socialization with other children or to never leave the Village property. As we traveled around Honduras and investigated other organizations that do what we do, we focused particularly on the ones that were "all inclusive", where the kids never left the property. We noticed right away the low social skills that these kids had, and we did not want that for our kids. Second, we knew if this was going to work, we needed to bring in paying students who would subsidize the educational costs of our kids. If it were out at the Village, which sits in the very humble village of Tegucigalpita, where many of the villagers survive as subsistence farmers, the locals would not be able to put their children in the school. However, if we put the school forty minutes away in Puerto Cortes, there was a chance that we could make it work.

We had a couple options in Puerto Cortes. We could build the school on the small piece of land that already held our church and medical clinic, or we could use the funds and purchase a piece of land that was behind our church. Since we could not do both, purchase the land and build the school, we were at an impasse. The owner of the land even agreed to give us a no interest loan for the land and allow us to make monthly payments until it was paid in full. In the end, we decided as a board that we could not take on any debt with our current situation and decided to turn the offer down.

We made plans to build the school structure on the three-quarter acre piece of land that was owned by our church and clinic in Puerto Cortes. This way the rooms could also serve as Sunday school classrooms for our church. It was a tall order. Construction began in January 2012. We planned a grand opening for the school in August of 2013, because we estimated it would take that long to build the two-story structure, find curriculum, advertise, enroll students, hire staff and do all that starting a school requires in eighteen months.

What actually happened was a miracle. Instead of eighteen months, eight months later, in August of 2012, we opened our doors. The Kwasneys were the right people for the job. Ashley began to get the word out regarding teachers and an ad was put in the local radio and television news and newspaper about the required positions. Over the next few months, we interviewed and hired several different people. We went with the Kwasneys to Tegucigalpa to meet with the Distributors of ACE curriculum. We decided to go with this curriculum for two reasons. It was a very Christ-centered curriculum that was developed to be a home school curriculum. It could be taught by anyone, including volunteers without teaching credentials.

In May students began to apply. They had to take a test which showed us where to place them scholastically. One of the main challenges with curriculum is that it is not cheap. Even though the paying students would be able to cover the cost of running the school, it would not cover the cost of our kid's curriculum. This would be an expense to the ministry of about $60,000.

We had to work very hard to come up with this amount of money out of nowhere. This was a very trying time for our ministry. Many supporters of H2H believed that we never should have gone forward with a school. Even though the public-school system had collapsed, many felt that it was better than nothing, and that we should focus on feeding our kids and not taking on a major capital project like a school. But we believed then and now that our kids are His Kids, and He wants His very best for them. While it did not seem practical in the human sense, it was what God was telling us to do.

Other people wondered why God did not give us all the money we needed to build the school, and also have the financial security we so desperately needed to feel safe and secure, to feel in control and on top of the situation, and to feel that we are doing the "responsible thing" with our kids and our ministry. It made more sense to me than anything else that I had heard in years. Everything that I had ever been taught about being an adult, about being responsible and being of sound mind was screaming, do what is right, hold back, pull out, be cautious. But God kept persistently saying, walk on the water. Even if it doesn't make sense, just do it anyway.

Everything seemed so chaotic, but we followed God out onto the water to wait and see what He would do. In August the school year started, and the excitement was high. Each day we got more students and the parents were also very excited. I started doing devotions with the kids each morning. As we did the diagnostic tests, not one child fell within their grade level. In fact, almost all of the kids fell very short, in some cases many grades levels behind in their math and in the sciences. We knew that they would be behind in their English, but math is a universal subject. It was disturbing to see high schoolers still counting on their fingers to do multiplication. The pitch that we were sold was that most of the kids could catch up to their grade levels within a year or two.

The school ended up being a haven. Each morning the kids walked into an area that had been thoroughly prayed over. They received prayer, worship and Bible study with me each morning. I taught them how to pray over our city, over their home, and over their country. We took each issue and brought it before the Lord. Then they also had devotions and worship in their classrooms. Our staff was very unified in one thing, that this was a place to lift kids up, whether they were from the Village or from town. These were the precious kids that the Lord had brought us to minister to and to disciple. We wanted the school to be a place where the kids not only learned about math, science, reading, and writing, but a place where they learned to be good people, model citizens and to serve God.

What really shocked us, especially in the first year, was that it was really the kids from the town who needed our love, more than the Village kids. There is one common thread that lies underneath the psyche of most Hondurans, and that is the feeling of being unimportant. As a poor country, most Hondurans struggle with self-worth, an unfortunate side effect of being born into an underprivileged country. In the local newspaper, there is a section called the "social" section. This ridiculous section of the newspaper concentrates on 2% of the entire country, those with loads of money! You can read all about their baby showers, weddings and luncheons. Who cares? Well, apparently Hondurans do. You're somebody if you are not poor. And if you can't be rich, then at least you do all that you can to look like you are. Hondurans work very hard to have a certain appearance, and it goes beyond pride. Their entire worth as a human being depends on it.

They do their best to put forth an appearance of wealth, even if they are completely faking it. In order to project themselves as wealthy, the first thing they do is remove themselves entirely from anything and anyone which might be thought of as poor. The culture of the country teaches kids that they should turn their noses up at the poor, dirty and uneducated. There is also a more sinister situation going on in Honduras. Since only a very small percentage of the population has money, they do their best to keep it that way. The education system is a joke. One of the laws is that if you start your education in public school you can never switch over to private. Their excuse for the law is that it is "unfair" to take a child who has only had a substandard education and put them into something more challenging, because their chances for failure in the new system would be high. But it is obvious that they fear anyone from the lower class somehow making their way up.

The society is set up in a way that the poor stay poor and the rich are safe on their high perches. Wealthy children are taught to think of themselves as "special" and better than others. But underneath what we have found are some very loved, but hurting, kids. Just like slavery in the United States taught children to hate and to fear, this kind of slavery in Honduras introduces a spirit of bitterness to the kids. They are often undisciplined, angry and disobedient. When they come to our school, we go right to work serving the poor. We teach the kids to become servants by working on serving others first. What they learn in our school is awesome!

Remember that most Hondurans live in victim mode. They see themselves as less than, and thus their mode of combating that is to try to pose as something more. We teach them to go down a different path. We teach them to achieve their self-worth by learning that Jesus loves them for who He made them to be and not what they can do or achieve. Since their low self-worth stems from feeling helpless, we try to show them how they can actually be heroes. They can learn to give and serve and thus overcome their feeling of powerlessness.

In 2012 we had the strange case of one of our boys named Freyson. A few years earlier, a woman came to the Village and told us she had a badly-behaved child she wanted us to take and "fix". We told her that we were not a correctional facility. We were a home for children who either had no one to care for them, or whose caregivers were abusing them in some way. She returned on several occasions and asked us to take her son, now saying that she worked all day and her son was only eight years old but was already being seduced by the gangs in the area. She was sure that within a few years he would be a full-fledged member.

After a few years of her constant insistence, we finally relented and took Freyson in. He was a beautiful, active child who looked more American than my own two daughters. He was a bit clingy but otherwise well behaved. Then one day, after her years of persistence, his mom showed up at the Village with a judge and said, "Okay thanks for your help. I think I will take my son back now." We couldn't believe what we were hearing! Was this a joke? When Freyson was told, he immediately went into panic mode, telling us please don't let them take me, I can't go back there. We told Freyson that he needed to let the judge know that he did not want to go back home and why. Freyson was taken to the courthouse to speak with the judge. We are not aware of what was spoken, but we do know that the judge ordered that Freyson would indeed go back home with his mom.

Over the next few weeks as his paperwork was prepared for him to go back home, Freyson cried and begged us not to make him go back. We told him that we were going to pray and watch what God would do, however they did come, and he did go back home to his mother. We were very sad about this and felt that we had really let this little man down. We continued to take our own advice, and we prayed. Then it came, the phone call from the family court saying, "You once had a young man in your home; however, his mother says that he has cried every day since he left. We have looked into the circumstances in his home and frankly we don't understand why he was allowed to go back! Could you please take him back to your home?" Oscar told her that we would take him under one circumstance, that the mother was never allowed to take him out again. The court agreed and Freyson came back home.

Day by day, hour by hour, and each New Year that went by, we could see God was proving His love for these kids. As I sit now, three years later and research through old emails and publications of the ministry, all I can see is progress, protection and provision. It's hard to even remember that all of this happened through years of famine! By this point we truly needed at least $5,000 more monthly just to be running well and at full capacity. But looking back, it was in those times that He carried us. God was, is, and always will be faithful.

Building the Mary Frenter Bilingual School in Puerto Cortes - 2012

Alana and Gerardo Ramirez with the kids in Tegucigalpita

Volunteers from the United States who taught at the Bilingual School

Volunteers reunited back in the United States

17

Honduras Is So Different From the USA

"And we know that all things work together for good to them that love God, to them who are the called according to his purpose." (Romans 8: 28)

For those of you who may not have spent a lot of time in a third world country, perhaps you are not aware of how public services operate. We have many volunteers from the United States in Honduras throughout the year, and there is always an "adjustment" that must happen when one comes to Honduras. One of the biggest adjustments is the heat. If you are from the South, as I am, then perhaps it's not that big of a change; however, as many of our volunteers come from the cold, wet Northwest, it is a real shock.

Honduras has a very different culture and mind set in many ways. It is very different from the United States, especially when going into town to make purchases. For instance, in the US, if you are building and want to purchase nails, you simply go to the hardware store, and the kind you need are normally sold by the pound. Not in Honduras. Here you go to the local hardware store, and they do not have the size or the kind that you need.

Now you must make the one-hour drive to San Pedro Sula. When you get there, you go into the hardware store and ask for the nails that you need. You are told to come back in an hour, and they will have your order ready. You return in an hour, and no one has even started on your order. Of course, they don't sell the nails by the pound, they are sold per nail. The salesclerk gathers the number of nails you need and brings that up to the place where you will be given an order form to fill out. The person at that counter will count out your nails one by one, however many hundreds of them there may be. Then they give you your order slip which you must now take to the pay booth, where they will count the nails once again.

A few years ago, I went to a teaching event about spiritual healing and deliverance. One of the ridiculous things that they taught was that when you go on missions trips you often will need to "clean" yourself of all the evil spiritual goop you pick up in the "heathen" nations you visit. At first, I thought, as if the United States is some pristine spiritual sanctuary!

I was spending some time in the United States and found myself very happy to get services promptly and well done, to drive around on roads with no potholes, and to not worry about getting shot at in a drive by shooting. As the time drew near for me to return to Honduras, I began to feel a twinge of "Oh boy, it's back to that mess now." I had become so drowned in comforts, that I had become spoiled. Immediately, I knew that was wrong thinking. I remembered the teaching on getting spiritual "goop" in a foreign country, and since I was in a foreign country, I began to cast off the spirits of laziness and entitlement that I had picked up while in the United States.

Another thing that is very different in Honduras is public utilities. The reality is that Honduras is very hot. The good news is I love very hot! The bad news is that the power goes out at least once a week in Honduras. Sometimes it is a scheduled power outage, and they are either conserving or servicing the equipment. When it is scheduled, you at least have the benefit of being told the day prior the hours the power will be turned off. Usually it is from 8:00 am to 5:00 pm. But often the power goes out because there is too much stress on the old, over-taxed system. Transformers blow out, thunderstorms blow through, wires snap, and these things happen often. Sometimes the power outages last only a few minutes, but many times they last several hours.

It is the same story for the city water service. Honduras receives copious amounts of rain on the north coast. For that reason, we have a beautiful tropical rainforest. Honduras can receive as much as 200 inches of rain per year. Sometimes I think it all falls on the same day. There are days when the rain comes down without mercy. Within a few hours the streets of downtown Puerto Cortes become rivers, and the rivers become deadly. I remember 2013 so well; it was the year the levy broke, literally.

It was November, right before Thanksgiving break, and a cold front came through northern Honduras. It rained all night in high gear. The next morning the kids came into school as normally scheduled; however, by 9:00 am it became clear that if we did not get them back home right away, they may be stuck in Puerto Cortes for the foreseeable future. We loaded them onto the bus for the Village, and not a moment too soon. The good news is that the kids made it home safe and sound. The bad news is that moments later a huge section of the road we had driven over was washed away.

Many rivers spilled over their banks and several hundred people lost their homes and were displaced. It was one of the moments when I wished we were a first responder organization. Several people in our church were forced out of their homes, and we had to help them relocate. During this massive storm, the pump system of the local public water company was damaged. So, the city water system was turned off. The really bad news was that it poured, then the heavens were completely shut up for the next month, not a drop of rain. The water was off for almost a month.

You have all heard about making lemonade when life gives you lemons, but bathing in the dirty river can get old. The blessing we had at the Village is that we have a well. The blessing we had at our home is that we have a swimming pool that we could use for toilets and cleaning. The challenge was huge at our volunteers' home, at the school, and of course at the homes of all our staff and church members. Our volunteers made lots of lemonade. True to their natures, they never complained. They collected the condensation off their air conditioners to bathe with.

The 2012-13 school year was our first official year of operation at the new bilingual school. Before the year began, we went through the processes of hiring several of our Honduras employees. Just a few weeks before the year started, we looked for housing for our volunteers and visited the rental home of a local pastor. The young man who came to show us the home was a very tall man by the name of Jorge, who was tattooed over much of his body. He was a nice young man who had recently given his life to the Lord, a life that had seen a lot of hard years in the world. Jorge was born in Honduras but moved with his family to the United States when he was only 3 years old. He spent a lot of his younger years in New York, thus had a strong New York accent. He then moved to Oklahoma and joined one of the most violent gangs in the United States. Jorge came back to Honduras after getting into trouble with the law and being deported. Now he was in Honduras, recently saved, and ready to serve the Lord at our school. Though it was very hot in Honduras, Jorge wore a long-sleeved shirt to work each day, so that his students did not have to look at his tattoos.

I will never forget that first orientation day. As each person went around introducing themselves, Jorge said, "I just want to say, that my life now belongs to Jesus, and all I want to do is serve him." Jorge had a wonderful, natural sense for working with children. He was able to see through to their real need. As I went to the parent teacher conferences to pick up the report cards for our kids, he was able to see through to the root of our kids. Many times, when one of our kids was not doing well, he could see into their real need and know why they weren't doing well. We were so blessed to have him teaching at our school.

We had another young man apply to work at the school by the name of Saul. Although we want the door to be open for anyone who wants to help, to have the opportunity at H2H, we usually only hire Christians to work with the organization. Saul was not born again at the time, but we felt very confident that he was the right man for the job. He had graduated high school in California and moved back to Honduras right after that. He had worked for another bilingual school in our area prior to applying for work with us. Saul was a gentle man and a great third grade teacher. At one point during morning devotions, Saul prayed and received Jesus.

18

A Testament to The Plans of God

"Now we have received, not the spirit of the world, but the spirit which is of God; that we might know the things that are freely given to us of God." (1 Corinthians 2:12)

It was late January 2013, and Kim Stephens was in Honduras with women from her church to run a women's conference. It was early Saturday morning, and I was with Rosa, our pastor's wife, at the church getting things prepared for the conference, when Sarah Matoon called me in tears. She had received a call the night before that both Saul and Jorge had been in a car accident. Saul died immediately, and Jorge died within a few days. While Jorge was in the hospital, our teachers visited him almost every day to see and pray for him. When Jorge passed away one week later, telling the children about their beloved teacher's passing was one of the hardest things we had to do. Both men were dearly loved by both the kids and the staff.

God was faithful and sent people to replace them in the classrooms. Earlier that year the Stephens family arrived. We had known Sean and Stephanie from a previous mission trip. They came to serve long-term at the Village, and Stephanie taught at the preschool at the Village. She graciously stepped into Saul's place at the school with her daughter Eliza and was a great source of healing for the kids. In addition, a young man from the Vancouver, Washington area came to volunteer for just a few months at the school. Brandon had no experience as a teacher and was actually a deep-sea fisherman in Alaska. He was a far cry from a fifth and sixth grade teacher, but he was just the right person that God wanted at the time. God used these people in amazing ways to show His great faithfulness.

One more of the young men who we had found living on the streets back in 2003 was now a married man. This time it was Norman. His brother came to the Village first and then asked us to take in his younger brother, Manuel. Both were living on the streets. Manuel and Norman spent their early years in a home with a loving mother, but a very harsh alcoholic dad. When they could no longer stand the abuse, they headed for the streets. Norman had been living behind the market in Puerto Cortes.

None of the original five boys wanted to come and live with us at first, but after the death of their friend Edgar, they realized that time was not on their side. When Norman was eighteen, he left the Village and started working to help his mom. However, he always stayed very close to the ministry. He continued to come to church and the youth group. He started dating his girlfriend Paola, even before he left H2H. In a small ceremony at our church, Oscar and I had the honor of marrying the couple. Norman and Paola continue to serve in the church today.

The school was doing very well, growing and gaining popularity in our community, so government regulations required that we add certain new classrooms. We prayed that we would get the $15,000 we needed to start to expand the school in order to meet the government regulations. One thing that you must understand about H2H is that we never sit around on our hands! If we are given $5 to buy some shoes, they are purchased on the way home from the bank. If we are given $100,000 to build a school, eight months later we are opening the school.

In December 2012, we got a visit from the couple who had donated the $100,000 for the school the previous year. I think all we had accomplished was a bit of a shock for them! We drove them to what was now an amazing center of education and discipleship for 200 children. I know they expected us to use the money for what it was intended, but I don't think they thought we would get it done so quickly. As a result of their visit, they donated the $50,000 we needed to put the entire third floor on the school building and open the school to more students. True to our nature, we began the work right away. Since school was in session, the work went on at night. From 6:00 pm to 6:00 am each night, the construction of the third floor went on with lightning speed. Within a few months, we had classrooms for 100 more students.

We were now in our third year of hosting Bruce Van Natta's Sweet Bread Ministries, Bruce Carlson, and St Luke's Lutheran Church for crusades in Puerto Cortes. After much prayer, we felt that the Lord really wanted us to do something different in 2013 with the crusade. We decided to invite two popular Spanish worship leaders to perform. The first night we invited Danny Berrios. If any of you know much about Spanish music, you will know that he has been a worship leader for more than two decades. On the second night, we invited Milton Valle, a charismatic worship leader from La Ceiba, Honduras.

Putting on a large crusade is no small task! The work starts months in advance. We rented the Puerto Cortes soccer stadium which seats 7,000 people, only because there was nothing bigger in town. On the first night of the crusade over 7,000 people packed the stadium and more than 2,000 were standing outside, unable to come in due to the lack of space. That afternoon, when Danny Berrios arrived from Miami, he was ill but was still able to sing. Bruce got up and gave his testimony, and then it was time for Bruce Carlson to go up and give the altar call.

The moment he got up to speak, the heavens broke open and a huge storm with driving rain began to fall. People began to leave the stadium. Bruce Van Natta ran up to the stage, grabbed the microphone, and told the people not to leave but to stay and pray. He began to rebuke the rain and each person present began to call out to God to stop the rain. There was no change, so Bruce said let's pray again and prayed. Then Paula Graves began to blow the shofar. She took a deep breath and blew for nearly fifteen seconds. By the time she had finished the rain stopped completely; what an incredible, merciful God!

The crusade went on and thousands came down on the field for salvation, infilling of the Holy Spirit, healing, and deliverance. One of our volunteers who did not really believe in this, came forward and was filled with the Holy Spirit. Just before we had to leave, Mary and my daughter Rachel were praying for some people who came up to them. Rachel was thirteen and was interpreting for Mary who did not speak Spanish. A mother with a young daughter, who appeared to be about five or six, and another older daughter, asked them to pray for the younger daughter to be able to speak, since she had been mute since birth. They prayed, and she left praising God out loud, and with her mother and sister in tears. Next, a young man with a broken collar bone approached them and asked for healing prayer. His arm was in a sling on the side of his broken collar bone, and as he spoke, he was in great pain and just barely moving the arm. As they prayed, he raised the arm in the sling to the heavens in thanks and praise to God.

The crusade had also been televised and was seen in 50,000 homes. When Oscar was at the bank the next week, the teller who served him told him that he had been in an accident and could not go to the crusade but watched it from his home. He said that the miracle of the rain stopping was remarkable. We firmly believe in miracles, but we don't want to call everything a miracle. After all, rain can just stop. It doesn't need to be an act of God.

However, the man at the bank told Oscar that from where he lives, he has a bird's eye view of the stadium. He said that he went outside to see what was happening. You could clearly see rain falling all over Puerto Cortes and something that looked like a hole over the Stadium where it was not raining. The truth is, he is not the only one who reported the very same thing, and it was also reported on the news. Many people said they could see an opening over the stadium that night where no rain was falling. However, in the rest of Puerto Cortes, it rained nonstop all night.

When the team was leaving, they ran into Danny Berrios at the airport. Danny was raised in a Baptist home, the son of a Baptist minister and admitted that he did not often believe in miracles. However, he became a believer that day! The next night he was signing at an outdoor concert in Siguatepeque, Honduras, when again it stated to rain, and the people began to leave. He told the crowd, "You can all leave but let me tell you what I saw last night." He encouraged the people to pray. He told us with joy that the same thing happened! The rain miraculously stopped, and the concert went on.

Yes, we are missionaries. Yes, we live in a very rural part of a very rural country, but farmers we are not! We have tried on many occasions but have failed every time. Our first attempt was back in the early days. It began with cows. We weren't looking for cows. We were looking for wood. All the finish work on the boys' home in Tegucigalpita, such as the door and window frames, is made of a precious wood that we bought from an elderly man who owns a large amount of property in Omoa County in northern Honduras. Northern Honduras is a tropical rain forest, so that basically means you can't cut a blade of grass without going through an act of congress.

After two months and hundreds of dollars spent going through court documents and attaining permissions, we now had the legal right to cut down a few trees in the jungle and build the doors and window frames at the Village. In the documentation, we had to present the precise location where the trees would be cut and prove that they would be replanted. The man's property in the documents was not measured in acres, but in kilometers. In our dealings with this gentleman, he told us that he also had cows and could sell us a pregnant one for the cost of only one cow. "Great," we thought, "we'll get two cows for the price of one." Well, it would have been if we had known what we were doing.

We brought the cow home that night and were now the proud owners of livestock. We were so excited about our new pet. The next morning our night watchman came upon a scene none of us wanted to see. Our seven- month pregnant mommy cow was lying dead in the field. She was big and clumsy and had stepped in a hole, fallen and broken her neck. She was still warm when the guard found her, so there was still time to butcher her and have her at least for her meat.

At that time, we did not have a freezer large enough to hold such a large animal. We had $400 dollars that had been sent down for something else, but due to the situation, we had to use the funds to purchase a second-hand freezer. It is still in the boy's house today. We are not farmers and apparently, nor are we butchers. The cow was crash butchered in a rush, so that she could be put into the freezer as soon as possible. The calf was already dead. Because the cow had not been hung to drain the blood, let's just say the meat was a bloody mess.

I share all of this to bring home the fact that we are horrible farmers. We also tried chickens, fish and pigs. All failed terribly for their own respective reasons. We have also done some planting, but the failure of the planting was not really our fault. In Tegucigalpita we have two strikes against us, even in farming. The first strike is the amount of rain that we get. Many crops cannot grow on land that is so wet. The second strike is, since we are just a few miles from the coast, once you go down a few feet, you hit sand. Go down another few fee,t and you hit saltwater.

Even so, we have always felt the need to be more self-sufficient at our Village. It would be good to know that even if all funding from donors stopped, we could still feed our kids. I think that God has the same thing in mind, and He shines through his church and through His people. It was this same year that we were contacted by two of our board members who are also involved with another organization called the Fellows Program. The Fellows Program is a discipleship program that serves college graduates who are seeking a way to use their education and training for the Kingdom of God. Each year the organization takes on a group of young men and women who desire to serve God, and the program even includes an overseas project. The project goal is to provide an overseas mission with a sustainable project that will benefit those that the ministry serves.

The Fellows Program offered to come to Honduras and do something wonderful for H2H. They were going to build an Aquaponics system at the Village. For those of you who are not familiar with what an Aquaponics system is, it is a garden system that grows vegetables in water fertilized by fish who live in the water of the system. It was May of 2013 when the first Fellows team came down to build and install the system. The young man who came down to assemble the system was an Aquaponics professional from California by the name of John.

John was a good-hearted guy who loved kids and loved what we were doing but did not yet know Jesus. One day as John was working very hard in the heat of the day, a very strange thing began to happen. John began to sweat blood, a very rare medical condition called hemosiderosis. It is caused by extreme stress on the body or mind. As you may remember, there was a very famous account of another case of hemosiderosis. It occurred when our Lord Jesus was in the garden knowing that he was soon going to face death.

John had never heard of this, and it was explained to him that Jesus had experienced the same thing. That night John spoke with his mother on the phone and explained that fact to her, extremely proud of the fact that he had also suffered for Jesus. By the end of the week Kim Stephens, who was in Honduras at the time, was sitting down at breakfast with John. She asked him if he wanted to give his heart to Jesus, and after all that he had seen, learned and felt throughout the week, his answer was yes. At the breakfast table he prayed with Kim and received Jesus in his heart. The next day our crusade team arrived in Honduras, and John was baptized in the Caribbean Sea.

An Aquaponics system is very complicated, and we had the blessing of having an actual agricultural specialist from Washington State advising us throughout the process. Deanne and Tim Converse are from the same town as Mary Frenter and worked closely with us on the system. They eventually came down the next year to help us get the system running well, and then came down several subsequent times to check on it. When running at full capacity, it will supply vegetables enough for the one hundred plus people who we feed each day. We are so thankful to Scott and Lisa Closner and the Fellows Program.

With nearly one hundred children, summer vacation from school can be a very dangerous time. When you start talking about two months with no school and nothing to do, it is a recipe for disaster. The school Easter break this year, we had made the mistake of not having an organized program for the children, but this time we were going to be smarter. We decided that we needed to run a summer camp program at the Village, and this was going to be our first year.

We started by hiring a man from our church who would be at the Village each day, Monday through Saturday. The camp was structured just like any summer camp a child might go to. It included recreation, teaching, Bible study, prayer, worship, soccer, art, music and outings to beaches, rivers, movies and museums. The program was a resounding success. As I write this, we are in the third year of running our summer camp at the Village. I am excited to see what God does this year!

Overall, 2013 was a remarkable testament to the plans that God has for these children. He has gone to great lengths to show us the plans that He has for them, and cost is not a factor to be considered. It is Easter season as I write this, and I am reminded of the great love of God. As we look at the needs of the kids and consider how to fulfill the commission that God gave to us for them, we remember what we were called to do. God did not ask us to put a roof over their heads, food in their mouths, and give them a bed to sleep in. God simply asked us to rescue them.

There is a huge difference, and we have always understood that. We were not to rescue them and be their saviors. Our role was to make sure they were not forced into the lives of their former destinies. This ministry serves a great purpose, and that is to show these remarkable children the living, breathing love of God. There is not a price tag that can be put on that. We are to show them that there was a day many, many centuries ago, when God needed to show His love for us. At that moment, cost was not an issue to be considered either. God will move any mountain, span any gap, and go any distance for you, His beloved. The Village, the school, and the clinic are all God's way of saying, "You are precious to Me, and I will go any distance to care for you." Thank you, Jesus for loving these kids.

Danny Berrios singing in Puerto Cortes, Honduras at the H2H Crusade

Puerto Cortes stadium and all the people who came to the crusade on the first day

Oscar and Bruce Van Natta sharing the word

Bruce Van Natta, Oscar, and Bruce Carlson

Women's Conference team at the San Pedro Sula airport

Women's Conference at the Heart to Heart church

Mary Frenter Bilingual School

19

A Peek at Christmas at the Village

"And thou shalt have joy and gladness; and many shall rejoice at his birth." (Luke 1:14)

What comes to mind when you hear the word Christmas? For me Christmas is simply magical. I think this goes back to some very precious childhood memories of the holiday. It didn't happen very often, maybe once or twice, but one of my most precious memories of Christmas is a party at my aunt's house. I must have been very young, but the event was fantastic. Each year I would get a new Christmas dress and some sort of Christmas jewelry. The party was usually the Saturday before Christmas and I was given my new dress and jewelry that very special night.

At the party, my aunt's house was beautifully decorated, and everyone was dressed to the nines. On the table was a glorious banquet of delicious foods. Christmas music was playing in the background and the atmosphere was full of a beautiful, welcoming spirit. Our family was all together, and we were celebrating the holiday and each other. We children were given hot chocolate with peppermint and marshmallows, and then at the end of the night we were all given our gifts. I will hold those memories in my heart for all my life.

Years later, after his kids had all moved out, I noticed that my dad didn't even put up a tree anymore. When I asked him at what point he become such a Scrooge, he told me the following, "Well honey, Christmas is for children. After you all moved on, I really didn't care to go to so much bother anymore." At this point I realized, all the clothes, the food, the parties and the magic had one purpose, and that was to bless the children in the family. It was to create wonderful memories for us.

It is vital to life and health to hold these good memories. In times of hardships and difficulties, they give us the strength of heart that we need to go on. God knows these kids have a multitude of bad memories to fill their minds, and it is put upon us to bring in good and precious memories to challenge them. Christmas is a perfect time to make that happen!

Each Christmas we have a goal in mind; let's make it awesome for our kids. Currently, we have ninety-eight children in our care, so we start planning many, many months before Christmas. Through various holiday fundraisers, we try to raise $100 per child or about $10,000. This covers several things: a new Christmas outfit and shoes for each kid, a Christmas and a New Year's meal, a gift for each kid, and fire works for our New Year's party. In November of each year, we host what we call the Christmas Prep and Quinceañera team. The team helps prepare the Christmas sacks with the gifts for each child and puts up Christmas trees and decorations at each house. Each year the kids get to make an ornament that they put on the trees as part of the decorations. Afterwards, I save the ornaments in hope to give them to the kids when they turn eighteen, so that they can share them with their own kids.

We also do Christmas cookies with Grandma Mary every year. Often when I ask the kids what their favorite time of year is, they say either Summer Soccer Camp or Christmas cookie time. Mary Frenter, our H2H President, was an elementary school teacher for nearly 36 years. She does something that most people would not even attempt. When the Christmas cookies are made, they are done in a forty-gallon plastic wash bin. Pounds and pounds of flour, sugar and butter are used and about 500 cookies are produced. It is a tremendous mess, but fantastic fun. As each child enters the cookie making room, they are doused with flour from head to toe. They are required to eat some of the dough and to lavishly give flour hugs to any and all participants. After the baking is done, amazing works of art are produced with the colored frostings and sprinkles which often bedecks their hair and faces as well.

Several days before Christmas, an amazing tradition gets started. One part of the traditional meals for Christmas in Honduras is tamales. If you have never made them, they are very labor intensive! Corn is grown, harvested and ground. It is then cooked down for several hours until it is made into a paste. Chickens are boiled in spices, and veggies are cooked. Then hundreds of banana leaves are cut, and the fun begins. It usually takes the effort of the entire Village to start assembling the wonderful "meal in a leaf" concoction. The first step is to open the banana leaves and spread the corn meal mix. Then you layer in the chicken and veggies, roll and tie up each individual tamale, and then boil them. We usually make about 300 to 400 tamales each Christmas.

Christmas in Honduras is usually celebrated on the night of the 24th rather than on the 25th. The festivities begin around noon on the 24th. What we normally do is break Christmas down mentally into two different time blocs. The noon to midnight section is for our kids under twelve years old, and from midnight on it turns into our teen party.

For all our kids thirteen and over, we first speak with them and ask for their help in giving the younger kids a wonderful Christmas. We divide them into groups and form teams. There is the set up and decoration team. There is the team that helps to serve the snack. Then there are the game crew, the dinner servers, the desert servers, and the cleanup crew. We ask them to help, with the understanding that they will be rewarded with an amazing teen party after midnight. The day starts with games designed for the younger kids. For the babies and toddlers, it is the Christmas Story time, for the girls it is a dance revolution dance off, and for the boys it is soccer or foosball.

Around 3:00 pm the kids break for a snack like candied apples. After snack, they go to shower and to prepare for the party, while the staff and volunteers get to work setting up. The older girls help the younger girls getting prepared with polished nails and toes, braided hair and best dresses. The boys all come in their new ties and freshly shined shoes. We do not allow our staff or volunteers to come in shorts or sweatpants. This is a very special event, and we want the kids to see that all our staff comes nicely dressed as well, since it is a formal dinner. We start the evening as all our kids are escorted into the gathering area dressed like little kings and queens. There is no hint of "street children" at this party; all are beloved children with a loving family. We start the evening with some Christmas songs, a prayer and then we all move to the dining area, where several tables have been decorated with candlelight and Christmas decorations. Then the meal is served.

The traditional Christmas meal in Honduras is pork leg with rice, salad and bread. We all sit together, all 150 or so of us, and have dinner together as a family. It is all our present kids, as well as many of our kids who grew up with us and now have families of their own, all of our house mommies, staff, volunteers, and even some church members. Then it is time to move back to our gathering area and each grade has a special song, dance or drama prepared. Then we bring out the Happy Birthday Jesus cake.

After the presentation, it's time to give the presents with the guest Santa. Each child is called up one by one to receive their gift bag of presents by the person dressed up as Santa. After the gifts are received and opened, we spread mats and blankets on the floor and play a Christmas movie while we serve popcorn and hot chocolate with peppermint and marshmallows. By the time the movie is over, it is near midnight and all the children twelve and under head to bed. The teens by this time have helped us tremendously and are in for a real treat themselves.

While the teen children are getting ready, a team of our volunteers return to the boy's house and decorate and prepare for an all-night teen party. We have music, photo booth, food and drinks, games, and activities. Usually the night wraps up and everyone is sent to bed around 4:00 am. It is a great deal of work but a truly amazing time.

We finish out the year with another wonderful celebration –

New Years! It begins with a very special meal of baked chicken. Then we light the bonfire, and it is time to start the s'mores. All of us go out to the basketball court and light firecrackers. At midnight we gather around the dining hall and count down to the New Year and then make a toast with all the kids. At this point the younger kids head to bed and the older children stay awake for the movie that was made highlighting the amazing things that God had done that year for our kids.

Christmas and New Year's will always be very special days in the life of our kids. It is a thrill and an honor to be part of something so joyful. Christmas celebrates the special gift of God's Son coming into the world, and the New Year celebrates new beginnings. We love to make this a special observance of all that means, not just on those days, but every day.

Group photo with the kids during Christmas - 2013

Christmas at the Children's Village (2018), Amy giving Christmas gifts to the kids, (l) with Osiris and (r) with Alejandra

Celebrating Christmas at the girl's house - 2013

20

God's Perfect Plan

"Trust in the Lord with all thine heart; and lean not unto thine own understanding. In all thy ways acknowledge him, and he shall direct thy paths."
(Proverbs 3:5-6)

In January of 2014, Gary and Ashley Kwasney, who had helped to start the school, were moving back to the United States. Mary Frenter and her husband Lyle were moving to Honduras, and Mary would be the new principal of the school. Mary never liked that we named our school the "Mary Frenter" bilingual school. She thought it should be named "Heart to Heart", like all our other endeavors. We only kept the name because years earlier we needed a name for the home school project we did at the Village and used her name for that. Later, things had changed in the school system, but it would take thousands of dollars to change the name, so it needed to stay. For the record, Mary still has not forgiven us.

Mary and Lyle moved into our home with us, so there were now twenty-one of us. Life in our home was wonderful! Shortly after that, Gerardo and Alana Ramirez moved down to Honduras to help at the school, as well as with our teenagers. We had known Gerardo for many years; he was a teenager in youth group at the church that we pastored in Washington State years before. It was a new church that had no musicians to lead worship, so Oscar asked sixteen-year-old Gerardo if he wanted to learn to play the bass.

Gerardo later went on to college to study music, and married Alana. He had come to Honduras many times over the years, but now he and Alana were living and serving full time in Honduras.

At that point Jordan, Gerardo, Alana and Mikaela, who was also a volunteer at the school, told us they wanted to return to Honduras the next year, but not as teachers. They wanted to have a different role in our kids' lives, especially the teens. What they wanted to do was to live with the kids and help our teens prepare for life outside of H2H. It was decided that Jordan, Gerardo and Alana would live at a rented home in Puerto Cortes, and our teen boys would live with them. Mikaela would live at the teen girls' home and run a discipleship program in our home. Everyone went back to the states in June of 2014 but returned to Honduras to initiate the programs in the fall of 2014.

It is amazing to see how God works everything out in His timing. Right before Mary moved down, H2H moved from a room in Mary's home, to a brand-new office space in Clackamas Oregon. Kim Stephens and Lisa Closner would be running the office. We did not know it at the time, but this all happened so that Mary could make the permanent move to Honduras. So, H2H ministry supporters, we are now officially Oregonians!

It was during the summer of 2014 that crisis hit Honduras yet again. Actually, it had hit years before. It was just that the effects were now coming to light. Each night on the news we heard the stories of the tens of thousands of migrant children from Central America who were making their way completely alone all the way to the US border. For many of the kids from Honduras it was a two-thousand-mile journey. By the end of the summer of 2014, it was estimated that nearly 100,000 children had left Honduras to make their way to the United States.

The journey is extremely dangerous. Many are taken by travel guides called "coyotes". For a very high fee they will take you from your home country to the United States. Many times, they are working with the criminal syndicates in Mexico, and unfortunately many of the kids don't make it. They are raped, killed, sold or just perish somewhere in the desert.

Why was this happening? Why would a mother or father send their child into almost guaranteed catastrophe? As I mentioned in previous chapters, Honduras had fallen into complete chaos a few years before and the country was now overrun by crime. Mothers had no way to protect their children. Local law enforcement was simply outgunned. Many people saw sending their children to the United States as their only option to save them. This was not the challenge of a handful of families, but literally tens of thousands.

That fall we met a family that was on the verge of that same desperate situation. Oscar worked on our coffee plantation in a village up in the mountains of Honduras and came to know this family. He understood that the mother wanted to send her children to the United States to keep them safe. Their father was a gang member and had been killed. The rival gang had gone to the mother and told her that the father owed them a debt. If she did not pay it, they would take the kids. Oscar told the mother not to send them; he offered her the option that they could come live with us. We were many hours away, and they would be safe. In the end the mother did not send them to the United States, and they are now living safely in our Village.

We were now into our seventh year of financial shortfall and had all but stopped taking in new kids. Our January medical team was invited by an old friend, Dr. Nelly Hernandez, to visit the public orphanage in San Pedro Sula where she worked. We went with all our volunteer staff and the medical personnel who were on the team. Three very special children grabbed our hearts on that trip. The first was a two-year-old little boy named Josué David. Josué had a very deformed lip and scars on his neck and chest when we met him. In fact, his bottom lip was completely gone in one section. He had to wear a bib when he ate and to protect his clothes from his constant drooling. We were told by the directors of the orphanage that his alcoholic father had bit his lip off in an angry rage. His neck and chest were covered in burn marks. It was apparent that this child had suffered very severe abuse.

We felt right away that Josué David belonged at H2H, so we made our request known to the government. They began to prepare his paperwork immediately. While on that visit we met two precious little girls, Alejandra and Osiris. Osiris had just arrived at the public orphanage two weeks earlier. She was a street kid in its purest form. Osiris lived off the garbage and whatever the locals would put into her begging little hands to eat and live. When the medical team treated Osiris, she had extreme anemia.

The other child we met that day was Alejandra. She stood out in the crowd as she was a blond haired blue eyed petite six-year-old. As we were leaving that day, Oscar struck up a conversation with this shy little girl, and she told him that her mom did not love her anymore and threw her away. She asked Oscar if he could go and find her mother and bring her back home. Oscar's heart was so broken. He said, "I don't know where to find your mother, but would you like to come live with me?" She told him, "No, I want to go with my mom, but she doesn't love me anymore." Oscar said, "But I can see if you can come and live with me." Crying this time, she said, "No, I don't want to go home with you. I want my mommy to love me and take me back home." Oscar told her, "Okay, maybe I will try to find your mom." He knew that we never could.

As Oscar was getting up to leave, the house mommies of the orphanage had called all the children to come eat lunch. As Alejandra turned to go to the lunchroom, she ran back to Oscar and said, "Okay, never mind, please take me home with you today. I hate this place." Now he had really done it! We could not just walk out the door with her; there was a legal process that would have to take place first. He told her that he would tell the people in charge to get all her things ready, and he would come back for her. She said, "Please no. Take me with you now. I don't want to be here." We simply could not do that, as much as we would like to. She latched herself onto Oscar and would not let go. The house mommies came and took her, screaming and crying, to the lunchroom. As we were walking out to the parking lot, you could hear her crying all the way from the lunchroom.

We could not allow that to happen, so we went to work right away. We applied to gain custody of Josué David, Alejandra and Osiris. The day finally came, about two months later, when the court called and told us to come pick them up. It was awesome to walk into the orphanage that day. We have done many rescues, but this felt especially great, because we had made a promise to a little girl who really needed to see an example of faithfulness. It was not a surprise; the children were all ready to leave. Both little girls were in pretty dresses, and Josué David was oblivious to the whole thing. When we walked through the doors and Alejandra and Osiris were standing there holding hands, the smile on Alejandra's face was enormous! Oscar put his arms around her and said, "What did I tell you? I told you I would be back for you."

Knowing Josué David's history, I was expecting him to be withdrawn and fearful of people, after all the degree of abuse he had suffered would make any child socially withdrawn and shy away from anyone, especially strangers. However, the ride home from the San Pedro Sula orphanage went completely to the contrary. We had the girls ride in the back seat, and Josué David rode in my lap. As he looked out the window, every animal we passed was a "vaca" or a cow. It could have been a horse, or a dog or a pig, but he pointed to it and said "vaca". We pulled into a fried chicken restaurant to get some lunch, and he ate and then joined the girls on the playground. When they arrived at the Village, he immediately found the soccer ball and went right to work kicking it around the playground. Since that day, all three children have done great. Operation Smile in Honduras has operated on Josué David's lip and will continue to do a few procedures over the next few years, but he is now able to eat and drink without a bib.

Volunteers, teen girls, Mary and Lyle Frenter with Amy

Amy with Alejandra, Osiris and Josué David

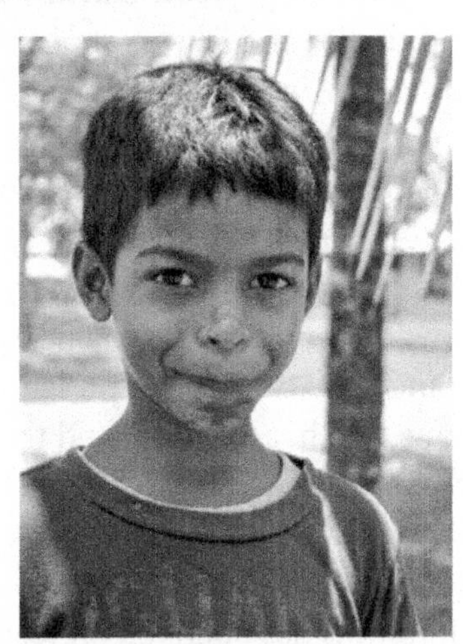

Josué David after surgery - 2018

Gerardo and Alana Ramirez

21
Jubilee Coffee

"But my God shall supply all your need according to his riches in glory by Christ Jesus." *(Philippians 4:19)*

Several year ago, one of our volunteer visitors and longtime friend of the ministry, Eric Smith, purchased a fifty-acre piece of property in the mountains in prime coffee country, so that H2H could grow coffee as a way to raise funds to sustain the ministry. Over the years, we developed this project and planted most of the area with coffee. In the fall of 2014, we got our first crop of coffee. Oscar went with the boys that summer to build a storage building and living quarters for the caretakers of the farm.

The vision for the coffee business is still in the works as I write this. We are hoping to export coffee to the states to further support the ministry. One of the great things about this vision is that we want it to be something that our children are involved in through each stage of the process. We want them to "own" this, as it is really theirs.

The process of producing coffee is very exciting from beginning to end. There is the growth and care of the plants, the picking and cleaning of the beans, the roasting and packaging of the coffee, and the sale and exporting. We want to offer our kids a business to be part of as they grow up and beyond. Some of our kids have expressed interest in studying business management, while others would like to study agriculture. We are excited to see what God is going to do with all of this.

It was now May 2014, and it was time for our Crusade team to return. In 2013, the crusade was large and ministered to many people, yet this year we felt God calling us into a very different direction. Several years ago, I was watching a worship service performed by a well-known worship group. The service was spectacular. The sound and lighting were perfect. The worship was spirit filled, and the place of worship was very inviting. As I began to worship and feel the amazement of such an event, a thought came into my head, "Why is it that only the wealthy can enjoy something like this?" We decided that this year, it would be an incredible idea to take the crusade to a community that would never be able to travel or afford to put on something like that. We decided to take the crusade to the poorest of the poor in the high mountain villages of Honduras. The two villages that we focused on were Concepción del Sur and Las Flores. Both were villages that we had a long history with and that we had ministered to several times in the past.

The crusade was both challenging and a breakthrough. There was quite a bit of strain between members of the team, but what was accomplished in the spirit realm was tremendous! To truly understand this, you must understand the spiritual, social and political backbone of many of these mountain communities. In both communities, you were either on one side or the other, and there was no middle ground. What I am referring to is religion and fighting for territory.

Nothing is sadder than seeing Christians and even pastors who will have nothing to do with each other at best, and fighting, gossiping about and dishonoring each other at worst. Churches fight over theology, and they fight over members. Those who are of a different denomination have nothing to do with those of other denominations. Even those in common denominations often fight over the "sheep". The situation is very sad, and it leaves the general public thinking, "Why bother?" One thing that the crusade did was call together all the local churches of every Christian denomination.

Even the members of our team said that this was an amazing

event. What happened the night before the crusade was nothing short of a miracle. Over seventy pastors and church leaders all gathered together crying out to God for forgiveness and revival. Each person spoke and asked for forgiveness of the other, and there were many hugs and handshakes. The pastors and leaders said that they had never seen or experienced anything like it. Pastors and leaders went up one by one and asked for forgiveness and reconciled with each other. At the crusade, several people were healed, and God did many miracles. Nearly 1,000 people received Jesus as their savior. We continue to work closely with each community and plan to send in teams and groups in the future who can make sure that things don't return to as they were, and that the new believers can be discipled.

We also had our first optometry team that year. Dr Jim Ogden of Goldendale, Washington had history with H2H many, many years ago. Lyle Frenter, Mary's husband, used to drive a school bus and six-year-old little Jim was one of his passengers. Dr Jim, who had done mission work in many other countries around the world, had now contacted H2H to see if we would be interested in him coming with a team from his church to provide glasses for our kids and for members of the church. We were interested!

Dr. Jim came with our old friends Gary and Sylvia Thacker with a group of mighty men and woman at his side and did eye exams on all our kids. For those who needed glasses, he let them choose from the many frames he had brought down, and then returned to the US and put their prescriptions in their chosen frames. A few weeks later all our kids who needed them had new glasses. Dr. Jim plans to come back to Honduras every other year to check our kid's eyes and update their glasses.

This was also another year for a glorious and fantastic first, our first wedding at the Village. We had married couples in the past, many of them our own kids, but no one up until that time had ever had their wedding at the Village. Our own Jensi came to live at the Village when she was twelve years old with her two younger sisters. She came to live with us due to abuse from her stepfather. Jensi went through high school, graduated from cosmetology school, and at nineteen was now working at our school as an office assistant. She met her boyfriend Angel two years earlier in the youth group at our church.

In September 2014, the couple decided to marry and wanted to do it at "home" at the Village. Now, I have been to many weddings in my lifetime, some of them I have even officiated, but this was the best, most beautiful wedding I had ever been to. I realize that I am biased, but let's look at the facts of this wonderful wedding. Jensi had a terrible life but had been brought to this place to be rescued and restored by God. God had done amazing things in her life and now He had brought a person into her life who knew everything about her, loved her very much, and the Village was where their life together would start.

The Village is a place like no other. The bonds of love and friendship that form there are deep. And though they are not blood family, the children raised there are bonded to each other in a much deeper way. Though they fight as all siblings do, when one laughs, all laugh, when one cries, all cry. They mourn their losses together, and they celebrate their victories together. When Jensi went down the aisle, she had her sisters and every girl who lived with her in the teen girl's discipleship house, every boy from the teen boy's discipleship house, as well as Angel's sisters, in the wedding. Almost every child in the Village had a special part in the celebration. The decorations were simple balloons, and the food was just chicken. It was nothing much to see until you looked beneath the surface. It was the beautiful arrangement of family and friends and supporters. I have never been in such an atmosphere of love and joy. Angel married into a huge, wonderful, and very strange family!

The ministry has grown and evolved in so many ways over the past sixteen years. It is amazing to look across the church on a Sunday morning and see two to three hundred amazing stories. Some were children who were once abused, abandoned or trafficked; some were people from the community who had been former gang members, prostitutes or alcoholics. While others were foreigners to this land who had been called from their comfortable homes in the United States or abroad to minister here. We were all together now, raising our hands, worshipping the Lord. What great things He had done and is still doing. We are all celebrating the greatness of our God saying there is surely no one like Him!

Jensi's and Angel's Wedding - 2014

"La Finca", building a cabin at the coffee plantation in the Santa Barbara mountains

22
Amy's Dream

"And they brought unto him also infants, that he would touch them: but when his disciples saw it, they rebuked them. But Jesus called them unto him, and said, Suffer little children to come unto me, and forbid them not: for of such is the kingdom of God." (Luke 18:15-16)

As I mentioned in previous chapters, in 2007 we were donated land in the mountain village of Concepción del Sur. When we were initially given the land, it was at a time that the ministry was so strapped financially that we could not even consider working there. But by 2013, the mayor was beginning to say that we really needed to move forward, as he had donated land that was purchased with community funds and donated it to us in good faith six years ago. We decided that we would bring most of our board up to the village to see for themselves, so that we could see how to proceed.

In November of 2013, we brought a large percentage of our board to the village. Many of them were not even board members back in 2007 when the land was donated and were not very connected to the idea. When we arrived, we met the mayor and saw the land. We decided to pray over the land and went out there with a young man who worked at the city hall. After the time of prayer, Kim and Rick asked the man if he knew Jesus and led him to the Lord right there on the mountain. The land we had been donated was beautiful, and you could see two different states from there. The elevation of Concepción del Sur is around 3,000 feet, so it is right at the foot of coffee country and offers stunning views of Honduras in all directions. Behind the city is Santa Barbara National Park at the top of Mount Santa Barbara, which stands at about 10,000 feet.

Four board members were on that team, and all felt that it was now time to move forward with developing Concepción del Sur. This was very hard on our board and this was one of the defining issues that caused our board to split in 2014. We were still hurting so badly financially and going into this new project appeared to be reckless to many supporters of H2H. But we knew that it was where God was leading us, and so we went forward.

The next team to visit Honduras was our crusade team. Bruce Van Natta and Tom and Paula Graves were on that team. We explained to them where the land came from and what the vision was. Initially, we offered to let Bruce's ministry Sweet Bread Ministries completely take it over. He told us he would pray about it and get back to us. Within a few weeks we did get an answer back from Bruce, but it was not an easy one. You see, so that tensions would ease on the board, we had hoped that we could wash our hands of Concepción del Sur. If someone else were to take it, then the problem would be solved. Bruce went right to prayer and fasting and asked for the help of his ministry partners to do the same.

Bruce called me one afternoon and told me he had an answer. Some of his prayer partners said that after a time of prayer that it should happen, while others said you are not to do it. Bruce felt the words were so conflicting that he needed further clarity, so he took another week to pray. What he felt that God revealed to him was that it needed to happen, but Bruce was not the one to spearhead it. It was H2H's to do. These were words I knew deep in my soul were true but had hoped were not. Not that I didn't want to go into Concepción del Sur, I most definitely did.

Before all this conflict had happened, Oscar had taken me up there, and I had a chance to stand alone on the property. Oscar had gone alone with the mayor to look at a river that ran down at the bottom of the property. I sat there on a rock, all alone in the middle of the property for about thirty minutes, and just prayed. In my spirit I could see hundreds of children running all over it, and the feeling that came over me was one of "safety". Whatever was going to happen at this place was going to be amazing, and God was giving it to Bruce. I mourned losing it, as I thought we had at that time. My only concern was that the board was already fractured, and tensions were running deep regarding our already strained budget. I knew this would push us over the edge.

As those words, yes it must be done, but you must do it, came out of Bruce's mouth, I felt both released and worried. Relieved in the sense of knowing that we were doing what God wanted us to do, but worried knowing that we had major financial and logistical issues to overcome. Did we have money when we first came down to Honduras? No. Did we have money when we broke ground on any of our buildings except for the school? No. So in the end, this was God's problem. Bruce told us that he thought that we should contact his friend Tom Stammon of Impact Ministries and see if we could work with him to getting funding for the building. After a series of meetings, Tom agreed that he wanted to work with us in finding the funding for building the new center. Pastor Tom and Paula sent funds to help get things started.

After working in the town for a while, we realized that the need in the town was a bit different than we had thought. Up until this point, we had believed we would replicate in Concepción del Sur a model of the ministry that we already had in Puerto Cortes. Concepción del Sur is a very small village in the mountains of Santa Barbara, Honduras. The population is not large, and the villagers are very poor. Many are farmers who often go away from their homes all day or for days at a time leave their small children at home alone.

This was the case of one family we met. The mayor was very concerned for this family, because the mother had run off with another man about a year before and the dad was left alone with his children. The oldest child was a ten-year-old girl who was now mom to the toddlers and babies in the family. The ten-year-old daughter was brought to meet us, and she looked and dressed like a sixteen-year-old girl. Her face was covered with makeup, and she had large hoop earrings in her ears. All of this was evidence that adulthood had been pushed on her way too early.

She told us that she enjoyed being "mom" in the home, but the mayor was very concerned as she was home alone for days at a time with small children. The girl was not in school and some of the neighbors felt that she was depressed and perhaps even suicidal. But the issue was, she had a dad and was not in danger. This family did not need to be split up. They just needed some help. The dad told us that the thought of losing his kids was more than he could handle. As we investigated the unique needs of this community, we realized that this was just one of many families like this in that community.

After a time of prayer for direction, we decided that we would move forward not as a children's home but as a place of refuge for those kids needing care while their parents were working. We decided that we would build a facility that would include a large area where we would meet to worship and pray with the kids. That area would also be an area where they could be served two good meals a day. We would build classrooms where the kids would have bible study, computer class, art class, music class, English class and whatever else we could give them that would enrich and bless their lives. We would also build a medical clinic, so that we could give them medical and dental care. It would be a daycare in a sense, where the kids could go to be cared for while their parents were at work.

We began the program in January of 2015 with rented building space donated by the City Hall. There were 180 children who received English class, computer class and daily devotionals with bible study, praise and worship and prayer. Today we are beginning construction of the center. We will be partnering with Impact Ministries and Sweet Bread Ministries to help what we hope will be hundreds of children in that community. This will be the first of what will be many Restoration Centers that we will build all over Honduras, wherever the Lord leads. Please pray with us that God will touch the hearts of the wounded Honduran children. Please pray that He would send laborers into the field and would give us the strength and the anointing to reach the ones that His heart breaks for.

We don't ever call it good enough. We don't sit on our hands. We don't take siestas! If there is even one more child out there in need, it is too many, and we will not rest until that child is taken care of. There was only one thing standing in the way of us going out and taking in and caring for even more children and that was money! You can only take in the amount you can feed right? When we could no longer stand the situation, we decided enough is enough. In November of 2014, our family left Honduras for six months to come to the states and make a major fundraising push for H2H ministries. We started on the east coast visiting our friends from Washington, D.C., Boston, New York, Tennessee, Louisiana, Washington, Oregon, Wisconsin and Missouri. Except for Easter Sunday, we spoke at a different church each weekend for six months.

I wish I could say that we found lots of support through this effort. I was saddened to see how little concern there was. We had hoped to raise the monthly income of the ministry by $5,000 a month, which would be an addition of about 100 new $50 per month sponsors. We did not think it would be too difficult, and we spoke to nearly 5,000 people over the six-month period. We did radio interviews and reached out to as many people as we could; however, the response was very sad. God began to put into my heart a message that we began to preach at each church we visited, and that was a message of compassion. I simply shared my testimony of how God called me from being a person who could not see the need, to being someone who understood it fully. At that point, the response became amazing!

I think I have always loved the church, but I loved her even more at that time. God gave me eyes to see what He saw in the church, power and potential. To realize that if the knowledge that Jesus Christ is savior lays in me, then in me lays the power to save the world! We become angry with God and ask, "If you are so great then why all the starving children, abuse and injustice in the world? Why don't you do something about it?" His response is, "I did do something about it. I created the force and the power to change it all, and that force and power is called the church. The truth is the church has enough resources, power, love and truth to be the answer to the hurting of the world." What happened? Could it be that compassion is no longer with us? Could it be that the enemy has robbed us of the victory that is ours?

I can say I love you and do nothing in response to that, but I can't say I have compassion for you and do nothing. Compassion is a gift that once received can never go back the other way. It changes you for life and turns you into someone different who no longer can look upon the injustices and do nothing. Compassion turns you into a person who no longer cares about building your own personal kingdom in this life, but rather spends your life to be the church in this dark hurting world.

Compassion is filled with holy anger! It is angry that the devil has taken so much territory. It declares in a loud, bold voice, not on my watch! Compassion is the ability to feel the hurt and need of others. And this big, beautiful body of Christ has lost the precious treasure of being the holders of compassion! As I walk into glorious worship centers with sound systems that cost thousands of dollars, yet I can't feed the orphans, I cry. "Where is the church?" But as we speak in the churches something becomes abundantly clear, the church is compassionate; it's just forgotten how to express it! Or rather, it has been stolen by the enemy. If He can get us so focused on "playing Church" and keeping up with the Joneses so to speak in church life, he knows we will stop giving to what is truly valuable. If you don't believe me then don't just take my word for it, let's look into the word of God.

In the book of Revelation, God speaks to the seven churches of Revelation. In chapters two and three, He is speaking to churches that actually existed in those times. However, most theologians agree that what is really being spoken of is a message to the church throughout the ages. In each church there is either a praise or a criticism for the church, often a mixture of both. However, there is one church that receives no praise and only rebuke. It is the church of Laodicea, the last church in the end times, or in other words, us! It's what He rebukes us for that hurts the most. He says in Chapter two verse 17: "You say I am rich. I have acquired wealth and do not need a thing, but you don't realize that you are wretched, pitiful, poor, blind and naked!" At this point the best thing we can do is not make excuses; we need to own that!

At some point I need to acknowledge that I too get sucked into the trap of thinking I can throw money at it and it will be fine. I too can believe that perhaps I have food today, because I have the favor of the Lord. What about the poor, faithful widow in Honduras who lives on faith to feed her children? Does she not have favor, or is it that the person with the "favor" isn't sharing? Oh, beautiful church of America, you DO have Gods favor. He has chosen us and given us the "favor" to be able to be a lighthouse to the rest of the world. He has heard our cry, "God, why won't you do something?" And He has said, "Here is more than enough for you, go and be my hands and feet." I think we missed the memo.

Oh, I understand, they are starving because they are "heathen" who worship idols, sacrifice their babies and practice abominations! I'm so glad that the United States doesn't do any of that! Who are we fooling? I understand that person is sick because of the sinful lifestyle they chose, so I must remember that I will be judged by the same measure that I judge. It's no surprise that it IS indeed sin that has come in and destroyed the nations that God loves so much. I know that many people are so deeply in bondage they refuse to give up the graven images they hold so dear, and we in the US lead the pack on that one. But isn't that the message of the bible? The wages of sin is death but the gift of God is eternal life! I never condone sin and have witnessed in my own personal life the consequences of sin. I agree that sin is the problem, and Jesus is the answer. Where is Jesus, and where is His church?

So back in the third chapter, you read my testimony. I prayed a prayer one day in the shower and asked God to soften my heart and let me hear the cry and see the need in a way that I was blinded to before. I pray that each person reading this book dare to do the same as me right now. I dream of a church that will one day rise up in the resurrection power of Jesus and bring down the gates of hell!

Can you dream with me and imagine a church that is filled with holy, living compassion? Then the church would be moved out of the pews and into the streets, not just in Honduras but right where we all live. Then the world could no longer deny this sleeping giant. It would be a game changer. The lost would be found, the sick would be healed, children would have a home and the hungry would be fed. Oh, God, that compassion would flood your church, especially here in American once again! Let's pray:

Lord, I thank you that you are a God of compassion. You saw me in my need and saved me. You called me to be your hands and feet. Help me know how to love like you loved. I don't just want to be a spectator; I want to be in the game. I don't want to just go through the motions. I want to see it and feel it. God, if there is something I am blind to, something I can't see, I don't want to be like that anymore. I want to know it and feel it in my heart. Lord let me be filled with compassion in Jesus' name.

Lord I pray for each person reading these words, that they would inspire, up lift, and move each heart. I pray that you would continue to build Your kingdom through each of us, and we will see your glory here on earth.

May our great God bless you all.

Amy

Epilogue

Mary Frenter

The events of H2H from 2015 to 2018 can be found on our webpage in the newsletters Amy and I wrote together each month. She had a unique "voice" to her writing that I love. It is quieted now until we meet again.

In those newsletters throughout the ensuing years, you will discover God's infinite love, care, compassion and comfort for His Kids in Honduras: the new kids, hand-picked by the Father to be part of this family; the losses we suffered with our twenty-six year old Maby to cancer, with our twelve year old Diana to the flu, and so many others of family and friends who have gone on ahead; the development of our Jubilee Coffee Company; the birth and growth of our three schools, the Divine Appointments God continues to bless us with; the many mission teams and supporters who continue to help this work of His each year; the successes of our amazing children as they enter adulthood and begin their own missions for God. It is a whole other book that, perhaps, someone will write someday.

But for now, we will close this "First 20 Years" chapter and, with the example set for us by our Amy and Oscar, we will go forward to continue the vision given to Oscar as a boy, to rescue, raise and restore the abused and abandoned children of Honduras.

When Amy got up off that bathroom floor just after God showed her the answer to her prayer for compassion, she never looked back. She stormed Honduras with this God-given compassion and with God's instruction clearly in her ears, she faced down every obstacle that was thrown in her path with unwavering faith and the compassion of God. She is the heart in H2H. She is the strongest, most faithful prayer warrior of all of us.

She always steered us to our knees in prayer when we faced insurmountable seeming challenges. She is the strongest and most faithful of all of us because of her intimate relationship with her Father God and Lord and Savior Jesus Christ.

I always refer to Amy and Oscar as Jesus with skin on. The word says in 1 Corinthians 13:12 "Now we see but a poor reflection as in a mirror; then we shall see face to face. Now I know in part; then I shall know fully, even as I am fully known." Amy has completed the journey of "but then, face to face" and "knowing also as she is known." My joy for her is unspeakable and full of glory as she beholds His face. We both loved the song, "I Can Only Imagine".

All the questions posed there are now answered for her. Standing beside Jesus, she will be there the moment God brings each of us home, to welcome us as she was welcomed the moment she stepped over. A close friend told me he was so angry with God for taking Amy now. Her answer, "Do not be angry with God. Nothing happens without His permissive will. I am fine. I am home. God's ministry H2H is going to be fine. Stir up your faith and rest in His arms of comfort for now. God's got this!"

To her children, Sarah and Rachel, and every one of you reading this who call her Mami, we may not have her physically here, but she is in your heart and mind forever. She will forever be an influence in your journey here on earth, and an example to you of what it means to be Christ's heart, hands, feet to all His family here on earth, of how to overcome, to never give up, of what accepting the cross of compassion to carry means and looks like. Her prayer for you was always, "Become what Jesus has in mind for you. Know Him by prayer and the word. Hide it in your heart. I expect each of you to have a ministry someday that will far outshine H2H. Put on the Armor or of God and get on with it. God never left me or forsook me. He will do the same for you. I am the blessed one. I am in the arms of my Savior. My peace and joy are complete. But all of you have your orders:

❖ Stay close to the source – Jesus Christ

❖ Listen to His commands,

❖ Know His word,

❖ Pray and obey

❖ Be fearless,

❖ Do NOT compromise what He has told you

❖ Measure your thoughts, words and actions by – WWJD? If He would not think, say or do it, don't you!"

To her beloved husband and all the rest of us, she says, "I expect every one of you to get up off your bathroom floor, dry your tears, and get on with whatever God has in mind for your oneness with Him, and the outflow of that in your service to others in His name. Get, and stay close to Him and LISTEN to His marching orders every day, whether you feel like it or not, and then OBEY them."

Over the years, as Amy and I would stand at the airport waiting for many of you reading this to arrive on teams, we would comment on how the crowd all around us was like a picture of heaven when one of His Saints arrives: All the people who are already there are standing on tiptoes, straining to see, looking expectantly for the face of their loved one to come through the arrivals door. Jesus is front and center, arms wide open, to welcome them. At first sight the new arrival runs and leaps into His loving arms, as all the rest gather around for a group hug. Amy, I believe that was what your first day in heaven was like, and His words to you were, "Well done, my good and faithful servant."

Rest well my daughter, my sister, my hero, my wise counsellor, my best friend. Your life made a miraculous difference for the Kingdom of God. You always prayed, "in Honduras, as it is in Heaven." Your memory, your name, will forever not only be remembered here, but will be a part of each of us privileged to have known you. We see your hand and heart in all H2H has, and will become, because of your unwavering obedience and literal God-given compassion for His Kids, from the day compassion came knocking and you opened the door, to the day you entered His presence.

I'll see you at the Grand Reunion. Save me a spot. I love you, Amy.

I will end this Epilogue as I began this book, with Amy's words of wisdom to us:

I am always reminded of how our Heavenly Father gets things done. It is not about buildings, homes, schools, clinics or churches, because one day all of these will fade away. It is Him building His dwelling place within us and doing what only He can do in us. It is Him saving, restoring and rebuilding what cannot be done with human hands. He does not build dollar to dollar or brick to brick. Our Father builds Heart to Heart." Amen.

Amabilia Ramos

Amy and Diana

Diana

Acknowledgements

Many thanks to all those who prayed us through the publishing of this book in English and Spanish both in Honduras and the United States:

To Dave and Paula Fester who, using their gifted abilities and professionalism, tirelessly proofed, edited, and created the published version, and set up the webpage to access all the online and hard copy versions of the book.

To Rick Stephens for editing, and copywriting.

To Luisa Palau, Ellen Hofmann, and Mary Frenter for the many rounds of additional proofing.

To Amy, who told our story in her beautiful voice that, while forever stilled, goes on in this work, ministering Jesus Christ to any who will listen.

To her children as well. Sarah, her eldest, now serves on the H2H Board of Directors, as does her youngest, Rachel who at age three, when she met someone new would say, "Do you know Jesus?" and if they said no she replied, "Would you like to?" and would proceed to lead them to salvation. These apples did not fall far from the tree.

And last but not least, to Amy's beloved husband Oscar, who was second only to Jesus in her heart. Oscar, along with their daughters, spent untold hours selecting the pictures that help tell the story, and translating it all into Spanish for our people in Honduras.

About Worldwide Heart to Heart

Worldwide Heart to Heart Ministries is a Christian nonprofit (501c3) organization whose sole purpose is to rescue and raise at-risk children living in Honduras. Our primary goal is to raise the children that God has given us, to help them become responsible adults who love Jesus, and for them to live as productive citizens. We provide a loving, Christ-centered environment where we aim to give the children an excellent education and a foundation for the future. Since our founding, we have raised over 150 children in our Children's Village and homes for teens and young adults.

In order to give our children the best education possible in an otherwise poor educational system, we built Spanish and Bilingual schools serving over 400 students and are seeing many of their graduates go on to excel in trades or to attend college. We also built a church, a medical & dental clinic, Amy's Dream Club, and other endeavors to bring hope and support to those in need. We also engage in outreach efforts to teach the kids about giving and operate a desperately needed food bank to feed the hungry. We are supported 100% by donations from people of many different Christian denominations.

Office:
PO Box 3275
Clackamas, OR 97015
Phone 503-427-0258
office@h2hcv.org

See more pictures, videos & interviews

h2hcv.org/book/more-content

h2hcv.org

facebook.com/WWH2H

Christian Speakers

The H2H Board of Directors, Oscar, Sarah, and Rachel Serrano, Rick Stephens, and Mary Frenter are available to speak at your church, school, or other special events to share what God is doing for His Kids in Honduras.

Mission Team Opportunities

Mission Outreach directed by the Holy Spirit is a major focus of most churches. We provide a mission field for short- and long-term teams to be used by God for His Kids in Honduras. Our team leaders are experienced and trained to make sure your team will be able to accomplish the goals you set for them.

After reading this record of God's work in Honduras through Worldwide Heart to Heart, if God has touched your heart to know more about how you can become involved or help, please contact us!

Worldwide Heart to Heart email:
office@h2hcv.org

Mary Frenter email:
maryf@h2hcv.org

Made in the USA
Monee, IL
18 February 2021